Shameless Liars

How Trump Defeated The Legacy Media And Made Them Irrelevant

Larry O'Connor

Forward by Kurt Schlichter

January 2025

Shameless Liars

Paperback Edition ISBN: 9798304045254

Copyright © 2025 Larry O'Connor

First edition

All rights reserved.

No part of this book may be used or reproduced by any means, graphic, electronic, or mechanical, including photocopying, recording, taping, or by any information storage retrieval system without the written permission of the publisher except in the case of brief quotations embodied in critical articles and reviews, provided proper attribution is given to the author.

Published by Over the Top Media, LLC

www.LarryVIP.com
info@LarryVIP.com
Written by Larry O'Connor
Cover design by Sean Salter
Edited by Meredith Dake-O'Connor

For Andrew Breitbart

None of this would have happened without you.

Shameless Liars

Table of Contents

Forward	1
Preface - George Stephanopoulos Pays the Piper	5
Part 1 - Who is the First Amendment Meant to Protect?	24
Chapter One - Thomas Paine: Anonymous Blogger	27
Chapter Two – Madison's Original Vision: We Are The Media	44
Chapter Three - The Myth of Objectivity: Breitbart Was Always Right	61
Part 2 - Debacle: The Media and the 2024 Election	77
Chapter Four - The Worst President of All Time	79
Chapter Five - Cheap Fakes and the Biden Decline	105
Chapter Six - Biden Falls And Can't Get Up	127
Chapter Seven - The Kamala Coup	141
Chapter Eight - Charlottesville, Bloodbath and Dictator on Day One	159
Chapter Nine - 60 Minutes Runs Out of Time	171
Chapter Ten - A Tale of Two Veeps	191
Chapter Eleven - Debate: Trump vs. ABC News	205
Chapter Twelve - Morning Joke: The Joe and Mika Show	223
Part 3 - New Rules	239
Chapter Thirteen - Trump Defeats Them All: The Victory Over the Media	241
Chapter Fourteen - The Podcast Election: Bypassing the Gatekeepers	255
Chapter Fifteen - I Stream, You Stream, We All Stream	271
Chapter Sixteen - We Are Now The Media	289
Acknowledgments	305
About Larry O'Connor	309

Forward

The title *Shameless Liars* is no accident; this is a book that may make you think and may make you laugh but comes from a place of moral clarity.

Larry O'Connor is angry, outraged at what's happened to our country and the deliberate failure of our institutions by people who've chosen to be rotten. And he should be angry. What the weirdos, losers, and mutations he writes about did to the United States we grew up in is an outrage. You might say that this tome is a cry of righteous indignation – and not coincidentally Larry's friend and inspiration, the late and great Andrew Breitbart, chose that title for his own book about people who are handed the greatest nation in human history and decided to turn it into a broke and woke mess.

2 | Shameless Liars

To understand why Larry, and Andrew as well, and even I, are so angry at the failures of the people we are supposed to be able to trust, you need to go back to another time and another place. Larry is a child of California in the 80s but with Midwestern roots. So am I. And, of course, Andrew was the quintessential Los Angeleno.

We three grew up in a time and place that was simply amazing. California in the 70s and 80s was a sun-dappled, palm tree-swaying alternative music paradise. Ronald Reagan was president and all was right with the world. America was at its pinnacle.

You young whippersnappers might not believe it, but our institutions worked back then. Even the media pretty much worked. Yeah, they were a bunch of liberals, but do you think Sam Donaldson would have conspired with Democrat poobahs to manufacture outrageous lie after outrageous lie? Can you imagine what the garrulous journalist would've done if somebody presumed to hand him a paper outlining the day's narrative?

Every regime journalist today sounds exactly the same because they're all taking their cues from the people they're supposed to be covering. Donaldson would've rolled up the daily talking points memo and made it a suppository. Do you think he would've pretended that Hunter's laptop was generated by a bunch of sweaty dudes with no necks toiling in a Moscow basement?

But the media hacks today not only did it, but they would do it again in a heartbeat. They're not just bad at their job. They're not even trying to do their job. Sure, they want the respect and admiration that you earn from being a neutral truth-teller who's not afraid to step on the powerful's toes, but these frauds are not neutral, and they're not truth-tellers, and they're shrimping those toes, as long as the digits are attached to a Democrat.

So, when Larry calls his book "Shameless Liars," he's doing it because he knows what the wrongdoers should do and he knows that they should be ashamed for not doing it. Like Andrew Breitbart before him, Larry's not mad because they're liberal. He's mad because they're liars.

They call themselves "journalists" when they're simply grubby propagandists doing the dirty work for an establishment that turned what was an incredible country a few decades ago into a giant mess.

But Larry is a Californian, which means he has hope. In November 2024, our people chose Morning in America over Brat Summer. That's a huge step, a turning point. Oh, we've got a long fight ahead of us, but we can win it. Like all classic Californians, Larry is an optimist. He knows we can get the America we grew up in back for the next generation. Larry's been fighting for that for the 15 years since we met through Andrew.

With "Shameless Liars," he is continuing the fight. And hopefully, Larry will inspire you to fix bayonets and join in the battle for our country's soul!

Kurt Schlichter
Manhattan Beach, California
January 2025

Preface - George Stephanopoulos Pays the Piper

"You've endorsed Donald Trump for president. Donald Trump has been found liable for rape by a jury. Donald Trump has been found liable for defaming the victim of that rape by a jury. It's been affirmed by a judge." - ABC News's George Stephanopoulos to Rep. Nancy Mace (R-SC), March 10, 2024

"ABC Agrees to Give $15 Million to Donald Trump's Presidential Library to Settle Defamation Lawsuit." - AP News, December 14, 2024

George Stephanopoulos wanted to make an impact on the political fortunes of former President Donald Trump when he began his interview with Congresswoman Nancy Mace of South Carolina that late winter Sunday morning. It was March 10, just five days after the "Super Tuesday" primaries laid to rest the notion that the quixotic campaign of former Gov. Nikki Haley had any chance of wrestling the Republican nomination away from the once and future president. Booking Mace on this episode of *This Week*, the fledgling Sunday Show from ABC News, was no accident. The 46-year-old had endorsed Trump in January and had endured withering criticism from the likes of Stephanopoulos and his elite media cohorts. After all, Mace was not only a fellow South Carolinian but also a woman. And one cannot turn one's back on the sisterhood. Especially to the benefit of Mr. Trump.

Stephanopoulos knew Haley was toast, effectively making this early Sunday morning his first chance to have an impact on the general election.

Trump had the nomination and it was now game-on for the November showdown between the most reviled man in American politics and the current occupant of 1600 Pennsylvania Avenue, President Joe Biden.

Biden was a Democrat and so, not coincidentally, was George.

Not just a registered, loyal Democrat; George was a political operative. A political operative who had functioned at the highest levels of power in American politics. He was Senior Advisor to the President - and briefly the White House

Communications Director during the Bill Clinton Administration of the 1990s.

That background made Stephanopoulos uniquely skilled in communicating strategic narratives to the benefit of Democrats and at the expense of Republicans. This, of course, made him a natural to transition from his White House job and eventually become the anchor of *Good Morning America* and *This Week*. As he prepared for the Mace interview that morning, Stephanopoulos must have rubbed his hands in anticipatory glee for his opportunity to employ all his political skills to begin the destruction of Donald Trump.

As a mainstay of the Hamptons/Manhattan social circuit, Stephanopoulos was an iconic representation of elite, conventional wisdom. And in 2024, the conventional, elite smart set knew full well that this presidential election would be determined by white, upper-middle-class suburban women.

Naturally, George had bought into this conventional wisdom. As previously stated, the smart set just *knew* this was true.

This is the other reason why the Mace booking was so important. She personally represented the exact demographic the Democrats were counting on to swing this election: Affluent, well-educated, women with an independent streak.

Stephanopoulos knew he could not get Mace to swing her support to Biden. That wasn't the plan. The plan was to press Mace on her support for Trump and challenge her for betraying the sisterhood.

The plan was to humiliate her and publicly shame her for not falling in line.

The plan was to send a clear signal to any other woman who might be on the fence in this election. The plan was to let them know that if they supported Trump like Mace, they would be subject to the same humiliation, shaming and bullying Stephanopoulos inflicted on the congresswoman.

The plan did not go well - for George.

Before Stephanopoulos introduced Mace to his viewers, he ran a clip of her announcement for Congress in 2019.

"For some of us who've been raped, it can take 25 years to get up the courage and talk about being a victim of rape," Mace said on the flashback video. " And the first thing that happens when a woman comes out in public and says she's been raped, what is the first thing out of someone's mouth? It's that it didn't happen. This is why women do not come forward. They are afraid."

The framing for the live encounter between Mace and the ABC News anchor was set. She had previously spoken eloquently and passionately about the pressure on rape victims to stay quiet, thus empowering their abusers. So, how could she possibly support Trump?

George, with the subtlety of an elephant's appendage, launched right into the grilling as the clip ended.

"You endorsed Donald Trump for president," he sneered. "Judges in two separate juries have found him liable for rape and for defaming a victim of that rape. How do you square your endorsement of Donald Trump with the testimony we just saw?"

What happened next was something George couldn't have prepared for. His producers couldn't have prepared him, either. Nor could the legion of staffers in the control booth who surely tried to scramble and whisper advice into his earpiece as Mace squared her shoulders and turned the narrative back on the Democrat operative.

The official transcript from ABC News is quite remarkable and is worth the small investment of time to read in its entirety from this point forward:

MACE: Well, I will tell you, I was raped at the age of 16, and any rape victim will tell you, I've lived for 30 years with an incredible amount of shame over being raped. I didn't come forward because of that judgment and shame that I felt.

And it's a shame that you will never feel George, and I'm not going to sit here on your show and be asked a question meant to shame me about another potential rape victim. I'm not going to do that.

STEPHANOPOULOS: It's actually not about shaming you. It's a question about Donald Trump.

MACE: No, you are shaming me.

STEPHANOPOULOS: You've endorsed Donald Trump for president.

MACE: Right.

STEPHANOPOULOS: Donald Trump has been found liable for rape by a jury. Donald Trump has been found liable for defaming the victim of that rape by a jury. It's been affirmed by a judge. He repeated --

MACE: It's not a criminal court case, number one. Number two, I live with shame, and you're asking me a question about my political choices trying to shame me as a rape victim and find it disgusting.

And quite frankly, E. Jean Carroll's comments when she did get the judgment joking about what she was going to buy, it doesn't -- it makes it harder for women to come forward when they make a mockery out of rape when they joke about it. It's not OK.

STEPHANOPOULOS: Doesn't it make it harder for women to come forward when they're defamed by presidential candidates?

MACE: It makes it harder when other women joked about it and she's joked about it. I find it offensive. And also I find it offensive that you are trying to shame me with this question.

STEPHANOPOULOS: I'm not trying to shame you at all. In fact --

MACE: You are. I have dealt with this for 30 years. You know how hard it was to tell my story five years ago when they were doing a fetal heartbeat bill, when there were no exceptions for rape, incest or life – or – and – rape or incest in there? I had to tell my story because no other woman was coming forward.

STEPHANOPOULOS: I'm just asking –

MACE: No rape victims were represented. And you're trying to shame me this morning.

STEPHANOPOULOS: I'm just asking you –

MACE: And I find it offensive. And this is why women won't come forward.

STEPHANOPOULOS: Women won't come forward because they're defamed by those who perpetrate rape. Donald Trump has been –

MACE: They are judged, and they're shamed, and you're trying to shame me this morning. I think it's disgusting.

STEPHANOPOULOS: I'm – I'm not – I'm not shaming you at all. I called you courageous.

MACE: I told my story. It took me 25 years to tell my story. I was judged for it. I still get judged for it today.

STEPHANOPOULOS: I'm asking you a very simple question, explain what –

MACE: And I answered it. You're shaming me for my political choices.

STEPHANOPOULOS: No, I'm not -- I'm asking you a question about why you endorsed someone who's been found liable for rape. Just answer the question.

MACE: It was not a criminal court. This was – this was a – it was a civil court.

STEPHANOPOULOS: It was a civil court that found him liable for rape.

MACE: And, by the way, she joked about the judgment and what she was going to do with all that money. And I find that offensive.

STEPHANOPOULOS: I'm asking you about the man who's –

MACE: But as a rape victim who's been shamed for years now because of her rape, you're trying to shame me again by asking me this political question.

STEPHANOPOULOS: You've -- you've repeated that – you've repeated that again and again and again.

MACE: I think it's offensive. As a woman, I find your – I find it offensive. For my political choices –

STEPHANOPOULOS: I'm asking –

MACE: I have endorsed the man that I believe is best for our country. It's not Joe Biden. And you looked at the dueling rallies yesterday in Georgia. Laken Riley's family was with Donald Trump. They weren't with Joe Biden. The same guy yesterday that apologized for calling her killer an illegal, who was an illegal. And here you are trying to shame a rape victim. I find it disgusting.

STEPHANOPOULOS: I mean you keep saying I'm shaming you. There's nothing I –

MACE: You are. The question – it is. It is.

STEPHANOPOULOS: How is the question asking you about a presidential candidate who's been --

MACE: You're asking a rape victim.

STEPHANOPOULOS: I'm – and there's no question about that. And you're -- you've courageously talked about that.

MACE: You're questioning my political choices because I've been raped. I think that's disgusting.

STEPHANOPOULOS: No, I'm questioning your political choices because you're supporting someone who's been found liable for rape.

MACE: You're shaming me. You're trying to shame me.

STEPHANOPOULOS: Actually, I'm not trying to shame you.

MACE: You are. That's exactly what you're doing.

STEPHANOPOULOS: You're not answering the question.

MACE: And I think it's disgusting.

STEPHANOPOULOS: Well, you're welcome to say that, but you also have to answer the question.

MACE: I did.

STEPHANOPOULOS: Why are you supporting someone who's been found liable for rape?

MACE: I just answered your question.

STEPHANOPOULOS: What is the answer?

MACE: He was not – he was not found guilty in a civil – in a criminal court of law. He -- it was a civil – it was sexual abuse. It wasn't actually rape, by the way. And E. Jenn Carroll joked about all the money she's going to get and made a mockery out of – out of this case. And I think that's offensive.

There is a reason why women don't come forward. And when you have someone who says that they're raped and they make a mockery out of this civil court judgment, it's offensive to other women. It makes it harder for other women to come forward when another woman has made a mockery of it.

STEPHANOPOULOS: You said women don't come forward because they are afraid. They are afraid because they are defamed by those who commit –

MACE: They're judged and shamed, like you're trying to shame me this morning.

STEPHANOPOULOS: They – they are – they are afraid to come forward, as you said, because they are defamed by those who commit the rape.

MACE: And they're judged.

STEPHANOPOULOS: That's what Donald Trump has been found guilty of doing.

MACE: He defended himself over that and denies that it ever happened. But he was not found guilty in a criminal court of law. It was a civil judgment over sexual abuse.

STEPHANOPOULOS: So is that the distinction you're making, a civil judgment is – is – is OK, but a criminal judgment is not?

MACE: This is different. And – and they didn't even input all of the evidence into the – the civil case either because some of the information she provided wasn't even accurate or correct. But to sit here and ask me, as a rape victim, too – to try to shame me for my political choices, is wrong. And I think it's offensive. And you --

STEPHANOPOULOS: You can -- you can repeat that again and again and again and again and again and I've done nothing to shame you.

MACE: And I'm going to because I find it deeply offensive.

STEPHANOPOULOS: You don't find it offensive that Donald Trump has been found liable for rape?

MACE: I find it offensive, as a rape victim, that you're trying to shame me for my political choices. And I've said again repeatedly, E. Jean Carroll has made a mockery out of rape by joking about it. I don't find that funny. Rape is not funny.

STEPHANOPOULOS: Well, you've -- you've made it perfectly clear.

MACE: Rape is serious.

STEPHANOPOULOS: You've made it perfectly clear, you're comfortable –

MACE: Rape is serious. It's not funny.

STEPHANOPOULOS: It is serious.

MACE: And it – it shouldn't be made a mockery of.

STEPHANOPOULOS: It is –

MACE: But if you want to defend a woman who made a mockery out of rape, then you go ahead and do that. I'm not going to do that.

STEPHANOPOULOS: Well, actually, what you're doing is defending a man who's been found liable for rape. I don't understand how you can do that.

MACE: Not in a criminal court of law. This was a civil judgment over sexual abuse, not rape, by the way, and she made a mockery out of it. So, which one are you going to --

STEPHANOPOULOS: Can we pull up *"The Washington Post"* headline right there? In fact, it has been shown to be rape. The judge affirmed that it was, in fact, rape. Donald Trump was found to have committed rape. That's just a fact.

MACE: That is a civil judgment, not a criminal court. They're two very different things and you know better.

STEPHANOPOULOS: Well, you've – I just showed you the facts right there.

MACE: You know better.

STEPHANOPOULOS: You show that you're very comfortable with what Donald Trump has done.

MACE: And what you've done is offensive to women who have been raped. What you've done this morning is offensive.

STEPHANOPOULOS: We'll let the viewers decide about that.

Wow. Not only did Mace turn the tables on her opponent and make the main focus on his obvious attempt to exploit her history as a sexual assault victim, but by consistently repeating her counter-attack, she baited Stephanopoulos into arrogantly repeating his accusation that Trump had been "found liable of rape." He clearly believed that by repeating the charge it would absolve him of his boorish behavior toward the congresswoman and he could continue to push a damaging narrative to turn those all-important suburban women against Trump.

George knew from his days on the campaign trail that it isn't good enough to deliver a winning campaign message just once. No, you've got to repeat it as much as possible to really deliver the talking point home and make it stick with the voters. It's called being "on message" and George was certainly "on message" this morning. He was so "on message" that he repeated the "found liable for rape" line seven times in less than six minutes.

Now that kind of messaging may seem tedious for the host of a Sunday show or any other interviewer, but George isn't really a TV host at moments like this. He's what he's always been: A political operative. And his political messaging was pure gold for the Biden campaign trying to send that "liable for rape" message to the suburban women they so desperately craved.

There was just one problem: Trump had not, in fact, been found liable for rape.

In fact, Mace showed more knowledge of the facts and journalistic integrity during the interview than the well-paid "newsman" for ABC. "It was sexual abuse. It wasn't actually rape, by the way," she fired back during the exchange. But, George was too driven to pay any attention to such things.

Mace was absolutely correct. The jury in the E. Jean Carroll case in fact found Trump liable for sexually abusing and defaming the plaintiff while specifically voting "No" on the question of whether Trump had "raped" her.

It may seem like semantics, but for political purposes the semantics are crucial. Democrats like Stephanopoulos were doing the work for the Biden team who really wanted that rape line out there as much as possible. *Seven times in less than six minutes!*

It's also more than a mere matter of semantics when one considers defamation law - which is exactly what Donald Trump and his attorneys considered upon seeing this political hit-job, cleverly disguised as an objective news segment, on one of America's largest broadcast networks. Within eight days, the lawsuit had been filed against ABC News and Stephanopoulos.

"Given Stephanopoulos's knowledge of the actual verdicts in Carroll I and Carroll II," the complaint read (referring to the past two lawsuits between Trump and his accuser), "and given his vast experience as a journalist, his repeated statements that [Trump] was found liable for rape were false, intentional, malicious, and designed to cause harm."

Indeed, the Trump legal team had also uncovered two previous occasions when Stephanopoulos accurately described the verdict in the Carroll case, not to mention the astounding reality that Mace, herself, corrected George live on air. But, the ~~Democrat activist~~ respected, award-winning journalist, ignored her and continued to repeat the "found liable for rape" charge.

It seemed like a slam dunk for a defamation suit… And it was.

On December 14, 2024, just days before the discovery process was set to begin, the parties announced a settlement in Trump's favor. ABC News would pay $15 million to the Trump Presidential Foundation and Museum. Additionally, Stephanopoulos would personally pay $1 million for Trump's legal expenses and a "statement of regret" would be published on the web version of the interview on the ABC News website. The settlement between the parties was entered on Dec. 13, 2024. It bore the signatures of Trump, ABC executives, and the letters "GRS" in the space for Stephanopoulos' signature.

It was a complete and total victory. Maybe even more influential than Trump's electoral victory six weeks prior. Trump had scored the biggest victory of his second term, more than a month from being inaugurated.

In a year of unpredictable, extraordinary, and unprecedented political events the successful defamation suit against a corporate media behemoth served as the perfect coda. Everything had changed and the propaganda-fueled legacy media was now officially on notice: Their lies and political activism, protected by the haughty armor of "journalism," would no longer have the dominating effect it had enjoyed for so many decades.

Once again, Trump's boldness delivered results not just on his own behalf, but for We the People. Our national political conversation would be exponentially improved as soon as high-profile, well-funded corporate-owned media conglomerates could no longer lie with abandon for their selfish political purposes.

Part 1 - Who is the First Amendment Meant to Protect?

Chapter One - Thomas Paine: Anonymous Blogger

"IT BEARS REMEMBERING that the purpose of a free press, like the purpose of free speech, is to nurture the mind, communicate ideas, challenge ideologies, share notions, inspire creativity, advocate and reinforce America's founding principles-that is, to contribute to a vigorous, productive, healthy, and happy individual and well-functioning civil society and republic." - Mark Levin, Unfreedom of the Press, *2019*

When you consider the First Amendment, you immediately recognize how our great founders made a perfectly clear and pure societal statement to the rest of humanity: That individual human beings were born with rights that could not be infringed by any government.

Those rights include the right to speak one's mind; To practice one's religious faith unobstructed by government intervention; To peacefully assemble; and To request redress from their elected leaders.

These are basic, fundamental human rights each individual should be free to exercise without tyrannical government obstruction.

The First Amendment is perfect.

Then, the Founders threw in one other right that doesn't quite seem like it fits. Indeed, it almost looks like an afterthought. Look at the text of the First Amendment. Can you see it? It sticks out a bit like a sore thumb.

*"Congress shall make no law respecting an establishment of religion, or prohibiting the free exercise thereof; or abridging the freedom of speech, **or of the press**; or the right of the people peaceably to assemble, and to petition the Government for a redress of grievances."*

While laying out the litany of Rights that Congress shall not be permitted to infringe upon, they threw in four little words:

"Or of the press"

Have you ever wondered why America's Founding Fathers crafted the First Amendment of the Constitution to include a special, exclusive, and inalienable right for reporters to be protected when they do their jobs? Or, for that matter, why did they ensure that same right extended to a handful of elite and wealthy owners of major media corporations?

Why did Madison, Hamilton, and Jay, overseen by Washington and advised by Franklin, ensure they protected their new nation's citizens from government tyranny over their right to speech and assembly and redress and religion, and also make sure the journalists and newspaper owners were also protected?

Why include the Press? Why ensure the rights of reporters? Why? Why protect wealthy owners of newspaper companies and future radio, television, and Big Tech conglomerates?

To put it simply, they didn't.

The protection of the press in the First Amendment stands shoulder to shoulder with those other fundamental rights because our founders recognized that it was to the great benefit of the *people* of the United States to ensure that the Press was uninfringed and uncorrupted by the fledgling government. The First Amendment protections of the press are designed to benefit *We the People*.

Our founders recognized that for the democratic process to work effectively in our brand-new constitutional republic, the people would need to be informed and educated in a way that was not controlled or worked in collusion with the government. The Press needed to be free - for all our sakes.

If we were to give the power to the people to utilize the tools of democracy to select their representatives in this republic, the people would need a free press so that they could make the most informed choices possible. A constitutional republic utilizing democracy to select its leaders can only work if the press remains free.

Freedom of the press is not for reporters and not for owners of news companies. Freedom of the Press is for you. Freedom of the press is for me. Freedom of the press is for *We the People.*

Understand that these patriotic founders just broke the chains of tyranny from an authoritarian monarchy where on the King's whim, the author of a critical column in the local daily pamphlet could be jailed without trial.

How could voters be expected to make sound and wise decisions at the ballot box if the free flow of information was encumbered by a tyrannical government? They couldn't. For the new constitutional republic to succeed in utilizing the democratic process, the press must be free.

The emphasis on Freedom of the Press for our founders may make more sense if we focus on the most influential and celebrated journalists of that time.

You already know his name: Thomas Paine.

Ironically, his most significant publication at the time of the revolution didn't bear his name when first published. *"Common Sense"* was indeed first published anonymously. When it was initially released in January 1776, the pamphlet was signed simply, "Written by an Englishman," without naming Thomas Paine as the author. This anonymity was partly due to the seditious nature of the content against the British Crown which could have led to repercussions for Paine if his identity had been known immediately. When Paine penned his pamphlet, his writing career had really just begun. Before that, he worked as a corset maker in his earlier years in England. He was later employed as an excise (tax) officer, a job he held in both England and briefly in America after his arrival.

By the time he wrote "Common Sense," Paine had made a bit of a name for himself as a writer, particularly with his editorial work in the "Pennsylvania Magazine," where he served as editor and contributed articles. But, he couldn't safely put his name on *"Common Sense"* lest he suffer severe political persecution. In a way, Thomas Paine was America's first and most important anonymous blogger.

Paine wrote in a straightforward, conversational style that made complex political ideas accessible to the common person. His language was free from the ornate rhetoric of the time which helped in reaching a broad audience, including those with little formal education.

One of the strongest parts of his work is Paine's argument for American independence from Britain. He posits that it is not only practical but *morally* right for America to sever ties with Britain, arguing that the colonies had matured beyond the need for British rule. His famous line, "The cause of America is in a great measure the cause of all mankind," encapsulates this universal appeal. Paine's denouncement of monarchy was groundbreaking. He argued that hereditary succession was inherently flawed, calling it "the most daring, impudent, and arbitrary imposition that ever was attempted upon mankind." This critique resonated with Enlightenment ideals about government by consent, not by birthright.

Paine made compelling economic arguments for independence, discussing how Britain was using America for its own benefit without reciprocation. He also touched on social issues, suggesting that independence would lead to a more equitable society, free from the burdens of supporting a distant, costly monarchy. Paine infused his arguments with moral and religious language, appealing to the public's sense of justice and divine providence. He argued that it was *God's intention* for humans to govern themselves, thus aligning the fight for independence with a divine mission. The pamphlet ends with a powerful call to action, urging Americans to unite for independence.

Paine's rhetoric was designed to motivate, with phrases like "We have it in our power to begin the world over again," inspiring a sense of urgency and possibility. These elements combine to make *"Common Sense"* not just a pivotal document in American history but also a seminal work in political philosophy, demonstrating Paine's ability to articulate revolutionary ideas in a way that was both persuasive and transformative. The impact and influence of Paine and *"Common Sense"* was swift and undeniably overwhelming.

Before *"Common Sense,"* many colonists still harbored loyalties to the British Crown or were ambivalent about independence. Paine's pamphlet shifted public opinion more decisively toward independence. His clear, persuasive arguments influenced key figures like Thomas Jefferson, who was in the process of drafting the Declaration of Independence. Jefferson's document echoes some of Paine's sentiments, particularly in the critique of monarchy. Benjamin Franklin was already an advocate for independence but appreciated Paine's ability to communicate complex ideas simply. He played a crucial role in getting "Common Sense" published and widely distributed, recognizing its potential to sway public opinion. Franklin's support helped ensure the pamphlet's influence.

Although John Adams later had a complex relationship with Paine, he recognized the pamphlet's impact. Adams noted that Paine's work had "a great effect" on the public mind, contributing to the momentum for independence. However, Adams also had criticisms of Paine's radicalism, showing the pamphlet's influence may not have been uniformly embraced but was certainly felt.

George Washington was known to have read and admired *"Common Sense."* He saw it as an effective tool in rallying the colonists. Washington's letters reflect his appreciation for Paine's ability to articulate the cause of independence in a way that motivated the populace and soldiers alike.

The pamphlet circulated widely among delegates in the Continental Congress, influencing discussions and decisions toward declaring independence. Its timing, just months before the Declaration of Independence, was critical in framing the debate and accelerating the move towards a formal break from Britain. *"Common Sense"* was not just a call for independence but also an articulation of republican ideals, which influenced the framing of American government. Its critique of monarchy bolstered arguments for a system of government by consent, which would shape the U.S. Constitution and the Bill of Rights. Paine's promotion of a government that serves the people's interests resonated with many of the Founding Fathers' own political philosophies.

Paine's moral and religious arguments provided a framework that many of the Founding Fathers could align with, even if they didn't agree with all his views. His assertion that independence was part of a divine plan for human liberty offered a compelling narrative that could unite diverse groups under the banner of a just cause. While not all Founding Fathers were equally influenced by Paine (some like Alexander Hamilton were more critical), *"Common Sense"* undeniably played a key role in crystallizing the argument for American independence, shaping public discourse, and providing intellectual ammunition for those advocating for a break from Britain.

Thomas Paine's influence extended beyond immediate political action into the foundational principles of the new nation. Yet, it was so dangerous and subversive he could not initially put his name to his work. Without the protection of the First Amendment, only secrecy and anonymity allowed this seminal document to be published and circulated. It may be hard to conceptualize life in the late 18th century colonies to perfectly understand how important it was to protect Thomas Paine, so let's attempt to make it a little more accessible.

Let's build a modern-day hypothetical.

Imagine we are just weeks before election day and a major American newspaper drops a bombshell investigative report involving the adult son of one of the presidential candidates. The candidate's son appears to be implicated in multitudes of illegal activities including illicit drug use, solicitation, and procuring of prostitutes (some, possibly below most state's definition of the age of consent) and good old-fashioned political corruption. All of these crimes are exposed through emails and text messages, either written by him or to him, and were discovered on the hard disk of the candidate's son's own personal computer. He personally handed over that computer to a repair shop and never picked it up, thus rendering the contents the legal property of the repair shop owner.

Now imagine this hypothetical, game-changing investigative report is ignored by all other news organizations unless they mention it while vilifying the publishers and authors of the report as propagandist liars working in tandem with America's foreign enemies. And further imagine social media platforms refusing to allow any person to link the article, lest they be implicated as aiding and abetting foreign interference in the

American election. Finally imagine, hypothetically of course, that these news organizations and social media companies were compelled to engage in censorship because law enforcement agents of the federal government directly and/or indirectly influenced them to do so under threat of criminal investigation by the American government.

You know, by now, the story we've just imagined.

The story of how the media ignored or downplayed the Hunter Biden laptop revolves around several key events and reactions during and after the 2020 U.S. presidential election.

On October 14, 2020, just weeks before the presidential election, investigative reporter Miranda Devine in the New York Post (founded, ironically, by one of the authors of the Constitution, Alexander Hamilton) published a story claiming that emails from a laptop purportedly belonging to Hunter Biden revealed his foreign business dealings and potential conflicts of interest involving his father, President Joe Biden. The laptop was alleged to have been left at a Delaware repair shop in 2019.

Several major media outlets and social media platforms initially responded with caution or outright skepticism. Social media giants like Twitter and Facebook took action to limit the spread of the story, citing concerns over the laptop's authenticity and the potential for it to be part of a Russian disinformation campaign. Many mainstream media outlets either ignored the story or reported on it with significant caveats due to concerns about its source.

Tax-payer subsidized National Public Radio, for example, explicitly stated they would not, "waste our time on stories that are not really stories," regarding the Hunter Biden laptop.

It took multi-billionaire Elon Musk's purchase of Twitter and his subsequent release of internal memos between former top executives and the Federal Bureau of Investigation for the truth of the government's bullying and intimidation tactics to be fully revealed.

Mark Zuckerberg, Founder and CEO of Meta/Facebook, later revealed to Joe Rogan that the FBI specifically warned them of the pending Hunter Biden story.

"The FBI, I think, basically came to us — some folks on our team — and was like, 'Hey, just so you know, like, you should be on high alert," he relayed to Rogan. "We thought that there was a lot of Russian propaganda in the 2016 election. We have it on notice that, basically, there's about to be some kind of dump that's similar to that. So just be vigilant.'"

"So we kind of just thought, hey, look, if the FBI — which, you know, I think, is a legitimate institution — is coming to us and telling us that we need to be on guard about something, then I want to take that seriously," he explained.

In their Dao Prize-winning investigative report, journalists Matt Taibbi, Bari Weiss, and Michael Shellenberger detailed how the FBI had censored the truth from the American people just weeks before election day. The FBI had been in communication with social media companies like Twitter and Facebook ahead of the 2020 election, warning them of potential foreign disinformation campaigns. There was evidence that the FBI specifically warned about a "hack-and-leak" operation involving Hunter Biden, which led to the social media platforms' initial suppression of the New York Post's story on the laptop.

FBI representatives were asked about the authenticity of the Hunter Biden laptop story, but they reportedly chose not to confirm or deny its legitimacy, thus allowing suppression by omission. An FBI employee inadvertently mentioned the laptop being "real" to Twitter, but this information was not widely shared or acted upon by the FBI publicly at the time. It turns out the FBI had a full working knowledge of the laptop's authenticity as the computer repair shop owner, John Paul Mac Isaac, turned the younger Biden's computer over to the agency in December 2019 - nearly a year before the New York Post published the story.

The narrative that the laptop could be part of a Russian disinformation operation was further fueled by an open letter from 51 former intelligence officials published by *Politico*. On October 20, just six days after the Post's story first ran, the 51 former intelligence officials, including some with active contracts with the CIA at the time, signed a letter suggesting that the Hunter Biden laptop story had "all the classic earmarks of a Russian information operation." It was later revealed in a House Judiciary Committee investigation that Antony Blinken, then a senior advisor to the Biden campaign, had contacted one of the letter's organizers, Michael Morell, to assemble the 51 names for the letter. Blinken would go on to become the United States Secretary of State after Biden's narrow victory that November.

That victory likely would not have happened without the FBI, CIA, and further government intimidation of these media companies. Indeed, a poll conducted by the Media Research Center in October 2021 (after the *New York Times*, Washington Post, CBS News and other legacy media brands finally got around to independently authenticating the laptop's contents) showed that 29.6% of respondents (nearly one third) said they would have been "less likely" to vote for Biden if they had been shown the truth of the Hunter Biden laptop as well as the "evidence Joe Biden lied about his knowledge of his son Hunter's overseas business dealings." That number includes 15.6% of Democrats saying they would have been less likely to vote for Biden in the 2020 election.

In that election, the margin of victory in the Electoral College was determined by the outcomes in three key battleground states:

- Arizona: Biden won by 10,457 votes.
- Georgia: Biden won by 11,779 votes.
- Wisconsin: Biden won by 20,682 votes.

If Trump had won these three states, he would have tied the Electoral College vote at 269, leading to a potential decision by the House of Representatives. Therefore, the total difference in votes that determined the Electoral College outcome was approximately 42,918 votes across these three states. And nearly 30% of voters would've been less likely to vote for Biden had the truth not been suppressed, censored, and misrepresented.

Under the guise of protecting the American presidential election from interference, the corporate media, influenced by the United States government, appears to have directly interfered with that very same election. *This* is why we need Freedom of the Press.

It's not there so Jim Acosta can keep his hard pass to the White House press conferences so he can wrestle a microphone away from a 20-something female staffer so he can berate the President of the United States. It's not there so billionaire Jeff Bezos can keep his fortune protected from defamation lawsuits as his Washington Post employees pen screed after screed falsely accusing the Trump campaign of colluding with Russians to steal the 2016 presidential election. And it's not there so CNN and the Washinton Post and myriad other propagandists can defame a high school student wearing a MAGA hat while being bullied by a Native American activist.

The protections reporters and their bosses enjoy from the First Amendment's press freedoms are not really there for them. They are ultimately there for us.

As we saw in the 2020 election, when the government can use their power to silence the truth from journalists, we all suffer. It has a direct and detrimental effect on our democratic process and ultimately on our Constitutional Republic. This is why we have Freedom of the Press.

Chapter Two – Madison's Original Vision: We Are The Media

James Madison, often considered the "Father of the Constitution," had significant contributions to the discussion on freedom of speech primarily through his involvement in drafting and advocating for the First Amendment.

On June 8, 1789, Madison presented his original proposal for what would become the First Amendment:

"The people shall not be deprived or abridged of their right to speak, to write, or to publish their sentiments; and the freedom of the press, as one of the great bulwarks of liberty, shall be inviolable."

This is worth contemplating at length.

"The people shall not be deprived or abridged of their right to speak, to write, or to publish their sentiments."

You see it, right?

Yes, Madison gets around to acknowledging that the freedom of the press is essential for liberty and must not be infringed upon, but he leads the entire thought with *our* rights. Not our right to "express our true selves" or to stand on a street corner warning that the end of the world is near or to publish hardcore pornography. He was quite specific and deliberate when listing our rights: Our right to speak, to write, and to *publish* our sentiments.

Publish our sentiments.

What was Madison getting at? Did he have some notion that we would all own a newspaper at some point? Or that we'd all be authors at some point in the future? Is this Madison having a strange "Andy Warhol Moment" with his colleagues?

"You know George, Ben, Alexander… it occurs to me that in the future everyone will be a publisher for fifteen minutes."

It's remarkable to ponder these words knowing that the right to speak, write and *publish* was foremost in Madison's thought process when contemplating the need to keep the government out of the business of policing speech.

It shows that the freedom of the press surely extends beyond the privileged few who are paid a wage to speak, write, and publish for an established news outlet. It also shows how those rights assigned to those privileged few were always designed to extend to each and every one of us and to benefit each and every one of us.

This language clearly extends all rights that reporters, editors, and publishers enjoy to amateur "bloggers" or citizen journalists who are often derided by mainstream media elites as "people in their pajamas pounding out screeds on their laptops." Bloggers and citizen journalists utilizing the tools available to them in the Wild West of modern communications have made significant impacts on news cycles over the past twenty years. And the professional elites hate it.

They want you to believe that freedom of the press should only extend to those with Journalism degrees from a college or university that bestow these suspect documents. Yet, it's noteworthy that America's first school of journalism wasn't established until 1908 at the University of Missouri. Are we to believe that for the first century of our nation's existence, press freedom was just sitting, waiting in the green room until it could finally be employed?

Nonsense.

No credentials, licenses, or pay stubs are required as proof that an American is eligible to be protected by press freedom. Madison's "[right] to publish their sentiments" language assigned to each citizen also amplifies the incredible, modern technology that we, the people currently enjoy and employ when communicating with each other and with all of humanity. Of course, I mean social media.

When we use Facebook or X (formerly Twitter) or YouTube or any other platform we are literally publishing our sentiments for the entire world to see. We are writing and publishing in a more powerful way than Thomas Paine ever imagined or "Poor Richard" Saunders when he published his Farmer's Almanac (with quite a bit of help from a guy named Benjamin.) The use of social media is implicitly protected by Madison's vision and language and it isn't even a close call.

That's why the American Government's role in censoring everyday American citizens from expressing their opinions and sharing information on these social media platforms was such an incredible betrayal of our First Amendment rights, including *our* freedom of the press. Let's explore another hypothetical thought experiment to illustrate exactly how bad it was and how unconstitutional our government behaved over the past several years.

Imagine, if you will, a global pandemic caused by a brand-new virus that has perplexed scientists and doctors worldwide. (Hopefully, this hypothetical exercise won't be too difficult for you to stretch your imagination skills into picturing this scenario.) Now imagine your national, public health agencies communicating conflicting and contradictory guidance and regulations that don't seem to make logical sense and force you into relinquishing basic freedoms for the sake of public health and safety, all in the name of science. Finally, imagine public health officials focusing almost entirely on the development of a vaccine to end the spread of the virus leaving hardly any discussion or research into treatment of the effects of the illnesses contracted due to viral infection leaving many patients and doctors to figure much of it out for themselves.

Can you even imagine such a crazy time?

Next in our scenario, you end up catching the bug and you feel awful. In fact, you're of a certain age and you've had some past issues with your lungs so you have what has been referred to as a "co-morbidity." In other words, this virus you've just caught could literally kill you. You go to your doctor and he suggests an antiviral medication he's had success with in the past. The medicine is called Ivermectin.

Now you're familiar with Ivermectin from hearing about it on the news. When some of those tin-foil hat aficionados were talking about Ivermectin they were mocked as if they were screaming about chemtrails and crop circles. Ivermectin, you were told, was for deworming sheep and horses. What are these lunatics thinking? This is how desperate people are, they're resorting to animal medicine to treat this mystery virus.

In August 2021, the FDA used its Twitter account to try to educate the unruly masses about their dangerous and harmful behavior. The official government-owned account tweeted, *"You are not a horse. You are not a cow. Seriously, y'all. Stop it."* The tweet was in response to reports of people self-medicating with Ivermectin to treat or prevent ~~COVID-19~~ sorry, this *hypothetical virus*, I mean. The tweet included a link to a page detailing why Ivermectin should not be used to treat or prevent this *hypothetical virus.*

Oh sure, you've heard about famous people getting results with the drug. That guy who calls play-by-play at the UFC fights, Joe Rogan... didn't he have some success with it? You do a quick search on your phone right there in the examination room about Joe Rogan and Ivermectin. The top result is a video from CNN. In the video, CNN referred to Ivermectin as a "horse dewormer" and "livestock drug." Weird framing considering Rogan claiming he was prescribed the *human* version of the drug by a doctor.

Wait, there's *a human version versus the livestock version? Why didn't the FDA make that distinction?* You think to yourself.

A chyron on the lower third of the screen during the CNN segment hosted by Erin Burnett read, "Joe Rogan says he has the *hypothetical virus*, taking livestock drug despite warnings." There's another CNN video. You click on it. It's Don Lemon's show with another chyron describing Rogan's actions as, "Joe Rogan, controversial podcast host, says he has the *hypothetical virus*, taking unproven deworming drug." Lemon also mentioned Rogan was taking "the deworming drug, Ivermectin, that has been touted by fringe right-wing groups." CNN's medical analyst Dr. Jonathan Reiner criticized Rogan's treatment regimen, calling it a "nonsense therapeutic mix" and pointing out that none of the drugs Rogan mentioned were recommended for non-hospitalized patients or for the treatment of viral infections like the *hypothetical virus*.

Suddenly you're starting to question your doctor's advice and his sanity. After all, you've done your research and, THIS... is CNN. The most trusted name in the news. Nonsense, your doctor tells you. Ivermectin has been around forever, he assures you. He's even had his own experience with it ten years ago when he caught what could've been Malaria while on an African safari. Ivermectin came to his rescue. Try it, he persuades you. Trust him, he implores. Against CNN's better judgment, you do.

What happens next is a miracle. You start feeling better within hours of taking the drug along with the rest of the medication regimen that Rogan spoke of. By the weekend you feel almost fully recovered. You were seriously afraid of your own mortality. You were the perfect candidate for death because of your age and comorbidity and you'd never felt as sick as this virus made you feel. You were terrified. And now, you're better.

You had to share this great news. You know that most of your Facebook friends are about your age. Surely some of them have the same comorbidities or dangers. If not, they may know someone who does. You have to let them know.

You take to Facebook:

Hey guys, I know these are scary times and we all know someone who's had a tragic reaction to this hypothetical virus. It's awful. I just had a terrible case of this hypothetical virus and I thought I was a goner.

But, here's some amazing news: I'm totally cured!

Now, I know this sounds crazy considering some of the news we've heard about it, but MY DOCTOR prescribed Ivermectin for me and it is a miracle drug! I'm not kidding.

MY DOCTOR says it's totally safe. He even takes it!

Listen, I'm not telling you what to do and I'm clearly not a doctor, but if you catch this hypothetical virus and you feel awful, ask your doctor about this stuff. Maybe for some reason, it's not right for you, I don't know, but ask your doctor and get their professional advice about Ivermectin.

All I can tell you is my personal experience and it totally worked for me.

Share this post on your Facebook page. You may save a life!

You hit "Publish."

Within about an hour, you get a notification from Facebook that you've violated their community guidelines and your post has been removed. Your account has been suspended pending further review. You're given a link to a page that has official government medical data and how it's being used as guidance for Facebook to monitor misinformation during the pandemic. It turns out, that the American government, through public health agencies, had put pressure on Facebook and every other social media company to delete posts like yours and suspend accounts. Facebook did this at the government's direction. The government, through their proxy, has censored your speech. They've intervened in your ability to **publish your sentiments**, just as James Madison had foreseen.

Okay, the hypothetical exercise is now over. (Seemed pretty real, didn't it?)

In 2024, after Republicans in the House of Representatives used their slim majority to conduct investigations into abuse of civil rights during the COVID-19 pandemic, Mark Zuckerberg Founder and CEO of Meta (the parent company of Facebook) made some astounding revelations. Zuckerberg stated that senior officials from the Biden administration, including some from the White House, "repeatedly pressured" Meta to "censor certain COVID-19 content" during the pandemic. This pressure included removing content such as humor and satire related to COVID-19, with officials expressing frustration when Meta did not comply.

Zuckerberg acknowledged that he believed this government pressure was wrong and expressed regret for not being more outspoken about it at the time. He also mentioned that Meta would push back if faced with similar demands in the future. Very real government censorship happened during this sorry time in our nation's history. It was not merely an infringement on freedom of speech. It was an infringement of our freedom of the press.

Our freedom of the press.

When an American citizen *publishes* a Facebook post as described above, they are not just speaking their mind, expressing themselves, or stating their opinion. They are reporting news.

Look at the hypothetical post again.

Other than the use of first-person which is not part of a normal style guide employed in your mainstream press outlet, it has all the hallmarks of a news report.

This happened. Then this happened. This expert was asked about it, and the expert said this. The results of the expert's advice was this. Take this information and share it. It might help someone who needs it.

The response to the censorship regime that trampled the rights of average Americans during the pandemic has been all too predictable.

"Oh, it was the fog of war."

"We were learning as we went along."

"Better safe than sorry."

"If we could save just one life by stopping dangerous misinformation…"

The real dangers of government-directed infringement on press freedom are amplified in that last, sorry excuse for the Biden Administration's authoritarian censorship regime.

Their fig leaf of "we were trying to save lives" presumes that someone's life would be in danger had they read your dangerous- hypothetical post about Ivermectin. But, of course, we now know that your post was not misinformation at all. In fact, we know now that if there was any misinformation in this scenario it was only that of the government and CNN.

So, in reality, under the guise of "better safe than sorry" and "we're just trying to save lives," the truth that you hypothetically reported was censored. This means that the people you were trying to communicate the facts about Ivermectin with never got to see your report. This means that it is almost certain that the very person you were reporting to, a person of a certain age with comorbidities who was suffering from COVID-19 and desperate for any help, never got to see the vital, truthful information you reported.

It means this person could have needlessly suffered. It most probably means this person died. They died because they were left uninformed. They died because the only information they were permitted to receive was the very wrong misinformation reported by CNN.

They were only allowed to see the government-approved misinformation that was promulgated under the guise of "better safe than sorry" and "if we can save just one life…" In this scenario, government censorship and infringement on press freedom most likely led to the suffering and deaths of untold American citizens. And they still pat themselves on the back and pretend they did the right thing.

Madison knew. He understood that for the people to truly have freedom, they need the unencumbered right "to speak, to write, or to publish their sentiments" and this freedom was not just for professional journalists like those who wallowed in Biden-allowed misinformation at CNN. Madison warned against gradual and silent encroachments on freedom by those in power, suggesting that these were more common and dangerous than sudden usurpations. It reflected his ongoing concern over the subtle erosion of speech rights. Madison constantly highlighted the importance of knowledge and public discourse for a free society. He believed that a well-informed populace was necessary for liberty, thereby linking freedom of speech directly to the education and enlightenment of citizens.

A quick epilogue on our not-so-hypothetical illustration of government censorship during the pandemic:

Further investigation revealed that Ivermectin was, indeed, safe and effective for many patients battling the effects of COVID-19.

CNN's chief medical correspondent, Dr. Sanjay Gupta, later acknowledged on "The Joe Rogan Experience" that CNN should not have referred to Ivermectin as "horse dewormer" when discussing Rogan's case, as he was taking the human version prescribed by a doctor. The identity of the government employee at the FDA who tweeted the mocking post for anyone taking the perfectly safe and effective drug has never been revealed and as of this book's publication date, not one person at the FDA has suffered any discipline for their actions related to public discourse over treatments of COVID-19.

Chapter Three - The Myth of Objectivity: Breitbart Was Always Right

"MSNBC and Rachel Maddow aren't the problem," Andrew Breitbart yelled down the phone line at me in 2010.

It wasn't *angry* yelling, mind you. It was *emphatic* yelling. Andrew wasn't angry, he was passionate. And his volume was designed to have the message hit home with me.

"Maddow and Olbermann and Ed Schultz tell the world exactly who they are. They're libs! Everyone knows it and they don't pretend to be anything else," he explained.

"They aren't the problem. The problem is CNN. The problem is Anderson Cooper," he continued.

"CNN still pretends to be objective. CNN still pretends to not have a bias. They pretend that they're just reporting the facts without any political slant while they're constantly lying about Republicans and sliming Republicans.

"Our fight isn't with the libs at MSNBC," he concluded, "it's with the closeted libs at CNN. They're the problem."

Breitbart was a visionary who began his career as Matt Drudge's editor at *The Drudge Report* before venturing out in 2009 with his own vision to change the media landscape. That same year, I began writing for him.

His first webpage was called *Big Hollywood* focusing on the entertainment industry. I was fortunate enough to have an article posted that first day. I wrote for him for free the entire year, a year that also saw the launch of two more websites, *Big Government* and Big *Journalism*, focusing on DC politics and the mainstream media, respectively.

By the middle of 2010, he had hired me full-time as the Editor of *Breitbart TV*, a video aggregating website. My job was to find and post at least 30 videos per day that would appeal to a right-of-center audience. Often, the best videos were of some outrageous and offensive thing said by a liberal commentator or news anchor on one of the broadcast or cable news stations.

On the day Andrew was emphatically explaining to me the distinction between Rachel Maddow being an obnoxious liberal and Jake Tapper doing the same but all the while pretending he's right down the middle, he had noticed that I had been posting a lot of content from unabashedly liberal MSNBC. To be honest, this stuff was low-hanging fruit.

It was easy to just watch MSNBC and get pissed off at something that Al Sharpton or Keith Olbermann said, snip the video, post on our site, and watch the clicks come in. But, of course, Andrew was right. It's not really news when a liberal acts like a liberal on a network designed by liberals, promoted as liberal, marketed as liberal and programmed specifically for a liberal audience.

No, the real story was hiding in the shadows at CNN. When Anderson Cooper allowed the mask to slip and show his disdain for the conservative, Tea Party movement by derisively referring to them as "Tea Baggers" (a sexual activity popular with gay men) that was way more important to exposing media bias than hearing Olbermann once again call Bill O'Reilly the "Worst Person in the wooorrrlllld" for the 50th time. It was that day that Andrew explained to me that "Objectivity" when it comes to journalists and the media was nothing but a fabricated myth. Indeed, a myth designed to camouflage the truth and subvert reality.

There was a time when nobody expected journalists (or reporters as they used to call themselves before their self-importance ballooned larger than the Good Year blimp) to be objective. Nobody even expected newspapers to refrain from taking a point of view. Indeed, it may surprise you to know that for the first hundred years of our country, newspapers were unabashedly proud to align themselves with one political party or the other. It was common knowledge that *this* newspaper was the Democrat paper while *that* was the Federalists (or the Whigs or, eventually, the Republicans.)

So, what happened? Why did we suddenly all feel the need to have our news delivered without a point of view? Why did newspapers decide that it was better to force this unnatural discipline upon their entire staff and pretend on a daily basis that they don't actually believe what they believe? Why do newspapers and broadcast networks feel the need to tell their audiences that they're something that they are not and they don't allow their personal, passionate, deeply held beliefs to affect their work when we all know that clearly, their personal, passionate deeply held beliefs obviously affect their work?

Obviously.

The idea of objectivity became a standard for American journalists in the late 19th and early 20th centuries. Before this period, American newspapers were often explicitly partisan, focusing on promoting a particular political viewpoint rather than aiming for neutrality. The shift towards objectivity was influenced by several factors.

It really all started with the Associated Press. The AP's decision to present itself as an objective, unbiased news outlet was not borne out of an altruistic desire to set its product above the partisan fray. Nor was it based on the moral preening we see today from the Jake Tappers of the world who try to establish themselves as more ideologically pure for delivering a non-partisan news presentation compared to that right-wing station getting all the ratings. No, the AP's move toward an objective, non-partisan presentation of news stories was really all about the almighty dollar. It was a profit-making scheme.

Founded in 1846, the AP was originally created by multiple New York newspaper editors to share the cost of transmitting news from the Mexican-American War via telegraph. This innovation allowed for much faster dissemination of news across vast distances, making news reporting more timely than ever before. The use of telegraphic communication meant stories could be shortened and focused on the essentials, leading to the development of a more concise and direct writing style. Fewer reporters were hired and fewer expenses were incurred while multiple papers could all share the reporting delivered by the team they mutually employed.

Lower costs, higher profits and fewer headaches with temperamental reporters.

In the 1890s, Associated Press editors realized that their potential market would be limited by partisanship. They aimed to provide news that could be used by *all* newspapers, thus fostering the need for an objective approach to news reporting. This was crucial since AP sought to reach a broad audience by leaving slanting and commentary to individual newspapers.

As journalism began to define itself as a professional occupation in the early 20th century, it attempted to adopt principles from the scientific method, which emphasized gathering and reporting facts without bias. This professionalization included special training and adherence to ethical principles, further normalizing objectivity as the foundation of "good" journalism. There were also more practical reasons for the shift toward a "just the facts" pretense in American journalism. Mostly driven by technology.

The telegraph, introduced in the mid-19th century, influenced journalism by necessitating a style of reporting that prioritized facts and brevity to suit the medium's constraints, thereby pushing journalists towards a more objective reporting style. With the consolidation of newspapers due to mergers and closures, especially from the 1920s onwards, surviving papers needed to appeal to a wider, less partisan audience, encouraging the adoption of objectivity as a so-called "professional ideal of objectivity" to increase readership across different political leanings. By the mid-20th century, objectivity had become a central tenet in the discourse of American journalism, aiming to distance reporting from editorializing and to provide a more fact-based narrative to the public.

Radio/TV host and author Mark Levin exposed the lie of the objectivity movement in American journalism in his seminal book "*Unfreedom of the Press.*" In the book, Levin argued that contemporary journalism has largely abandoned the pursuit of objectivity in favor of promoting a progressive political agenda. He writes that journalists today engage in "social activism, progressive group-think, Democratic Party partisanship, opinion and propaganda passed off as news, the staging of pseudo-events, self-censorship, bias by omission, and outright falsehoods," instead of traditional objective fact-gathering and reporting. Levin points out that the move toward the "objectivity standard" in American journalism also coincided (maybe not so coincidentally) in the late 19th and early 20th centuries with the insidiously destructive "Progressive Era."

At the same time journalists were urged to adopt the aforementioned "scientific approach" to journalism to minimize personal and cultural biases, other American institutions like academia, entertainment, and politics were being infiltrated by anti-American progressives looking to undermine the foundational values the country was built upon. The stated ideal of objective reporting was corrupted over time, especially from the 1960s onwards, when journalism took a turn towards social activism following significant socio-political upheaval. Reporters (now routinely referring to themselves as journalists) see themselves no longer as objective witnesses to world events but as active participants in shaping those very events they were meant to cover. From the civil rights movement to the Vietnam War culminating in the largely media-fueled Watergate scandal, journalists saw themselves as the actual catalysts who ended segregation, a war, and even a presidency.

This utopian ideal of unbiased and objective reporting from elite news organizations sounds all well and good, except one must remember the reporters, editors, publishers, and even these photographers all have strong points of view and the temptation to inject their perspective into their reporting frequently emerged too hard to resist. In reality, the camouflage of objectivity ultimately provided the perfect disguise for what actually amounted to blatant editorializing bordering on outright activism. When called out on their ethical lapses, the denizens of America's newsrooms could continue to claim innocence and feign outrage over the mere suggestion that any of them had operated in any way other than ethically pure and completely objective. And they could always count on their colleagues from the competing newspapers to stand up for them and defend their sacred honor as newsmen. After all, they were all in on the same game. If there was attack on one reporter or newspaper, the reporters would circle the wagons to protect and defend their "colleague."

This common cause was not borne out of any personal loyalty to their fellow reporters who they privately probably envied and loathed. No, the defense of the "craft" of journalism was really grounded in a much more basic sense of self–survival. Reporters will always defend each other because they know that when they are exposed and attacked, their "dear colleagues" will be right there to defend them like they were there for their "dear colleagues" This is why they gather every year at black tie gala after black tie gala to award themselves for being so outstanding at what they do. It builds the family trust. It reinforces the code.

But then, in 2016, something happened. Something they didn't expect: Donald Trump won the presidential election. Or, more to the point, Hillary Clinton *lost* the presidential election.

In 2016, only two major American newspapers endorsed Trump for the presidency, fifty-seven endorsed Clinton. On election day, the *New York Times* predicted Clinton had an 85% chance of winning the White House while the Huffington Post inched their predictor scale up to an astonishing 98%. The media's collective dismissal of Trump and embrace of the historic victory Clinton was poised to enjoy was so palpable that you'd be hard-pressed in the days leading up to election night to find any analyst on television giving voice to the possibility that Trump could accomplish what he ultimately did.

The best you may have seen would've been a moment when the analysts may concede that Trump had a narrow "path to victory" but they'd immediately snap back into line and predict the Clinton win.

In the end, they were all wrong.

The impact on the media was actually much worse than their realization that they had predicted the outcome incorrectly. No, they saw the election results as something much worse. They saw Trump's victory as a direct repudiation of their influence on political events.

And they were right.

There was a time when the mind-meld of DC/NYC political journalists would declare collectively that any given candidate was toast and, for the most part, their declaration would come true. Trump was declared dead or unqualified or disqualified multiple times in the 2016 election but he never had the good graces to do what the media wanted him to do and get off the stage.

On election night, the monolith that is the political media class was sure that the voters would finally give Trump the message they'd been trying to give him for months. But the voters didn't do what the media expected them to do. No, they didn't do what the media *told* them to do. The voters rose up and defeated Clinton, the chosen one of the media elite, and sounded off to the political establishment with one, strong, unison shout: "THIS is how pissed off we are!"

If you're the elite media, the day after that election, you'd probably re-think your entire understanding of the country and the voters you pretend to report about on a daily basis. You'd probably spend a lot of time with self-reflection wondering how you could have missed what was growing in the very country you call home - especially considering your *job* is to know what voters want and how elections are going. You'd probably spend considerable time fixing what was wrong in your profession so you could better serve your employer and the audience you are meant to inform. Yup.

You'd probably do that because you're a humble, rational, and wise individual. You're not in the elite media.

After the 2016 election, the media did not engage in any of that self-reflection or humble analysis leading to self-improvement. They took a very different approach. After Trump's victory, several media outlets shifted their approach from their cosplaying traditional objectivity towards outright advocacy journalism and taking even more explicit political stances.

Rather than re-group and re-tool their newsrooms with some diversity of opinions and political perspectives, these stalwart news agencies decided that their real problem was they had tried to report on Trump too fairly and too even-handedly. Dean Baquet, the executive editor of the *New York Times* at the time, admitted in a 2019 staff meeting that his newsroom had been built around covering the phony Trump-Russia Collusion story. He noted that they had to regroup and shift resources after the Robert Mueller report had not conclusively proven collusion, suggesting a pivot in their editorial focus from what was essentially a central narrative of their coverage during Trump's early presidency. Think of it: The entire newsroom built around chasing a phony narrative for the sole purpose of bringing down Trump and his presidency.

At *The Washington Post,* the masthead was changed to include the sanctimonious and ironically ripe-for-ridicule slogan: "Democracy Dies in Darkness." Meanwhile, their Captain Queeg-like pursuit of the very same Russia Collusion scandal that wasn't employed quite a bit of "Darkness" while claiming to resuscitate "Democracy." WaPo reported an unprecedented number of unverified and anonymously sourced leaks from within the government, many of which never actually paid off what the un-named, unknown and shrouded in darkness sources claimed they were delivering.

CNN went through the biggest transformation in terms of dropping all pretense of objectivity. Their re-invention of the "most trusted name in news" into just a weaker, less entertaining version of MSNBC was a complete debacle.

Their ratings plummeted and many of their stars (Don Lemon, Chris Cuomo, and Jim Acosta in particular) became so unhinged in their anti-Trump coverage that any pretense of objectivity could no longer be manufactured.

These shifts were often justified by some within these organizations as necessary responses to what they perceived as extraordinary political circumstances, with Trump's presidency seen as a threat to democratic norms or truth itself.

Wesley Lowery, a former Washington Post reporter, said, "The act of journalism, no matter how much we may fetishize the idea of objectivity, requires a series, a pyramid, of subjective decision-making."

Lewis Raven Wallace, who was fired from public radio in 2017, wrote in a Medium post titled "Objectivity is dead, and I'm okay with it," suggesting that traditional notions of journalistic objectivity were no longer viable or necessary in the context of Trump's presidency. Wallace emphasized the challenges of suppressing moral judgments for the sake of neutrality, particularly during such politically charged times.

Masha Gessen, a writer for The New Yorker, argued that "if we're going to have an ideal, then moral clarity would be a much better guiding ideal for journalism than objectivity." Gessen posited that journalism was inherently political and that the practice of striving for objectivity could normalize behaviors or events that should be critically examined, especially during the Trump era.

Jay Rosen, a New York University journalism professor, described journalistic objectivity as a "surface upon which enemies of the press wield their war against the truth," indicating that the concept has been used as a tool to discredit journalists rather than fostering truth or fairness in reporting.

In the end, Trump got them to drop their facade of objectivity and show the world who they had always been: The myth of objectivity had been exposed. Breitbart would've been proud.

Part 2 - Debacle: The Media and the 2024 Election

Chapter Four - The Worst President of All Time

In the *next* chapter, we will explore the most scandalous and blatant example of political deception and propaganda perpetrated on the American people in our history: The cover-up of President Joe Biden's debilitated health and cognitive deterioration.

In reality, though, the lies about his decline are actually just the icing on the cake of a presidency that was incredibly awful. Biden oversaw every conceivable type of failure, from economic to foreign policy to national security - and the media lied about all of it. Those historic failures, and the media's active role in lying about them, will be the focus of *this* chapter.

To fully appreciate the Soviet-like level of deception perpetrated by the media working hand in glove with Team Biden, we must explore the myriad of failures, scandals, and incompetence that encompassed the four years from 2021 through 2024 and how the political press in America lied, covered-up, and gas-lit the American people to prop up their man and to stop Donald Trump.

Covid lies

Biden took office with the promise that he would, "shut down the virus, not the country." He claimed in the final Presidential debate in October 2020, referring to the COVID-19 pandemic and the shut-down protocols that had ground the American economy to a virtual standstill. This soundbite was played far and wide in the American media and was propped up as a "defining moment" for Biden trying to draw a clear distinction between his approach and that of President Trump.

The media portrayed it as Biden's promise to tackle the virus head-on while focusing on keeping the economy operational. We were told this was Biden's attempt to reassure voters about both health and economic stability. Sources like Business Insider emphasized this line as part of Biden's strategy to counter Trump's claims about a potential economic catastrophe under Biden's presidency. Nowhere in the not-at-all critical coverage of this focus-group-tested one-liner did any of the legacy media teleprompter readers point out that it was overwhelmingly *Democrat*-run states that were still engaged in draconian shut-downs in the Fall of 2020 (California, Illinois, New Yor, etc.) and it was *Republican*-governed states like Florida, Texas, and Tennessee that had begun the re-opening process.

Trump had been using his bully pulpit to try to get states and corporations to re-open and return to normalcy within weeks of the mid-March "15 Days to Slow the Spread" guidelines Anthony Fauci and the media bullied him into adopting and promoting. Trump began pushing for the reopening of the U.S. economy during the COVID-19 pandemic in April 2020. On April 16, 2020, he announced the "Opening Up America Again" guidelines, which provided a phased approach for states to begin reopening based on public health criteria. Trump's push to re-open was met with derision, criticism, and outright propaganda.

Many media outlets claimed the guidelines were premature, given the ongoing spread of the virus and they trotted out "experts" to fear-mongers about masking, social distancing, and classroom conditions. Of course, the masking, social distancing, and classroom protocols have all since been debunked and revealed as pure fiction but at the time, any challenge to them was met with outright censorship and claims that "children would die" if anyone suggested that schools could re-open. Biden's claim he would "shut down the virus, not the country" was premised on an outright false assertion, and more maddeningly, when he took office, he did virtually nothing to "shut down the virus" (whatever the hell that means) or to open up the economy.

He allowed the powerful teachers' unions to dictate school shutdown policies at the Department of Education. He used none of his political influence on his fellow Democrats to loosen protocols in their states and his only major actions in the first months of his presidency involved a budget-busting, inflation-accelerating, $1.9 trillion stimulus payment scheme called the "American Rescue Plan Act." This he did alongside a vaccine strategy that was riddled with lies in its own right.

Vaccine Lies

Many legacy media propagandists love to repeat the Biden Administration's political talking point that the 46th president "inherited a broken economy" from his predecessor. This suggests, of course, that Trump's economy was a disaster (it wasn't) and it neglects to assign the proper blame for the COVID shutdowns: To the Communist Chinese (and the Democrat governors in love with their "emergency powers" to dictate health protocols.)In truth, though, there is one major thing that Biden did inherit from Trump: The RMNA shots that were widely (yet erroneously) described as a COVID vaccine. Biden took office with the shots already in production and a distribution plan already drawn up. And right on cue, the Biden team immediately lied about the shot and the plan.

White House Chief of Staff Ron Klain stated that the process to distribute the vaccine "did not really exist" when they came into the White House, which implied a lack of a distribution strategy from the Trump administration. It was an outright lie. There were indeed plans in place, including the framework of Trump's Operation Warp Speed (OWS) that was adopted and expanded by Biden's Administration leading to a full roll-out of the shots right on Trump's original schedule. An entire volume of books will be written about OWS and the impact of the shots on public health and individuals who contracted the COVID-19 virus, but to claim that Trump had no plan or that his plan was not successful is just plain fiction.

OWS significantly accelerated the development and approval process of COVID-19 shots, achieving in less than a year what typically takes many years. Multiple "vaccines" were developed, tested, and authorized for emergency use within this timeframe. This rapid development has been likened to historic "moonshot" projects like the Manhattan Project or the Apollo Program, highlighting its unprecedented speed and scale. While taking credit for the development of the COVID serums, (a tweet from the official White House Twitter account in May 2022 claimed that "there was no vaccine available" when Biden took office - an outright lie) Biden also made outrageous false claims about the effectiveness of the shot. That misled the American people into taking the "vaccine" under the false promise that it would stop the spread and prevent individuals from being infected.

During a CNN town hall in July 2021, Biden said, "If you're vaccinated, you're not going to be hospitalized, you're not going to be in the ICU unit, and you are not going to die." He also said, "You're not going to get COVID if you have these vaccinations." President Biden would regularly claim the "vaccines would stop the virus," despite the scientific evidence that he knew at the time about what the shots would actually do. Biden doubled-down on the lies with the oft-repeated propaganda slogan: "The only pandemic we have is among the unvaccinated," first publicly stated by Biden in July 2021. Dr. Rochelle Walensky, the Director of the Centers for Disease Control and Prevention (CDC), said during a briefing that same month, "This is becoming a pandemic of the unvaccinated."

In December 2021, addressing the Omicron variant, Biden warned that "for the unvaccinated, we are looking at a winter of severe illness and death — if you're unvaccinated — for themselves, their families, and the hospitals they'll soon overwhelm." The "pandemic of the unvaccinated" lie was insidious and divisive. It personally amplified the fearmongering that "the only reason we still have a pandemic is because of those anti-vax, anti-science neanderthals who refuse to get the shot." These lies, repeated by the President of the United States and authority figures in his administration fostered a bigotry against individuals who refused to take the yet-to-be-fully-tested serum and further divided the nation.

Unvaccinated individuals faced social ostracism in various forms. People were barred from social gatherings, including family events and celebrations. Unvaccinated individuals were treated as outcasts and faced mockery or had death wishes expressed towards them. Some unvaccinated individuals reported being denied medical treatment or facing discrimination in healthcare settings. Numerous states and businesses implemented policies that barred unvaccinated people from various public and private spaces. This included restrictions in restaurants, gyms, and other public venues, often requiring proof of vaccination for entry. There were also instances where unvaccinated individuals couldn't travel or fly without a vaccination card, effectively barring them from certain activities.

Biden's "pandemic of the unvaccinated" rhetoric created a palpable scapegoating effect that vilified, ostracized, and demonized individuals for making their own private, personal health decisions. The American media spent virtually no time exploring the true facts about the effectiveness of the shots and instead repeated Biden's mantra without question or challenge.

The lie took hold: If your kids are suffering because schools are closed, if your business is suffering because of the shutdown, if a loved one is infected and is suffering from the disease: It's all because of those anti-vaxers… it's all *their* fault.

The demonization of political opponents

The scapegoating and demonization of so-called "anti-vaxers" was nothing new for Joe Biden and certainly didn't serve as an exception for his public statements as president. Indeed, Biden's most memorable speeches during his lamentable time in the White House were delivered to purposefully divide us as a people and as a nation. During his victory speech in November 2020, Biden said, "I pledge to be a president who seeks not to divide but to unify; who doesn't see red states and blue states, only sees the United States."

In his inaugural address in January 2021, he emphasized unity multiple times, saying, "With unity, we can do great things. Important things. We can right wrongs. We can put people to work in good jobs. We can teach our children in safe schools. We can overcome this deadly virus."

Biden reiterated his apparent commitment to unity during his 2022 State of the Union address, emphasizing the need for Americans to see each other not as enemies but as neighbors, despite political differences. This was all fake, phony rhetoric, and hardly any of these bromides were followed up with any actual attempt to understand, listen to, or even meet with his political opponents. Instead, at every possible opportunity, he used his bully pulpit to bully Americans who dared to support Donald Trump and the Republican party. Despicably, each of his attacks on Republicans and Trump supporters was consistently framed within the false assertion that he was actually trying to unite us all, while dividing us even further.

The perfect example of Biden's "unite through division and demonization" tactic was a speech he delivered in front of Independence Hall in Philadelphia in September 2022. The iconic American edifice was bathed in blood-red lighting with Biden ranting at a brightly-lit podium in front of the famous bell tower. The lighting and stage-craft projected an image straight out of 1930's authoritarian Europe as Biden, fists clenched, often shouting, called for unity, but only unity under his authority. He was also flanked by Marine sentries who, because of the dramatic lighting, appeared in a somewhat threatening silhouette. The imagery underscored his message's urgency: He described the moment as an "inflection point" for America, where the nation must decide its future direction.

Biden yelled, "As I stand here tonight, equality and democracy are under assault. We do ourselves no favors to pretend otherwise." He spoke about the foundational principles of American democracy, linking them to the historical events that shaped the nation, like abolition, the Civil War, suffrage, and civil rights. He then explicitly linked the fight over slavery and civil rights with Trump and the GOP. Biden explicitly named Donald Trump and referred to "MAGA Republicans" as an extremist threat to the nation's democracy. He said, "Donald Trump and the MAGA Republicans represent an extremism that threatens the very foundations of our republic." He contrasted this with what he called "mainstream Republicans," stating his willingness to work with them. Then, after calling his political opponent and the 79 million Americans who voted for him an existential threat to our nation, he laughingly called for unity.

"I'm asking our nation to come together, unite behind the single purpose of defending our democracy regardless of your ideology." He emphasized the need to reject political violence and to uphold democratic principles, implying that Trump and MAGA were violent and undemocratic. This speech was framed not just as a policy statement but as a battle for the "soul of the nation," directly linking the upcoming midterm elections to the defense of democratic values. It wasn't a unifying speech in any way whatsoever. His "blood-soaked Independence Hall" diatribe had no unifying effect at all, except within the cozy confines of Biden's all-to-reliable legacy media. Media outlets highlighted Biden's speech as a stark warning about the threats to democracy from "MAGA Republicans." The speech was described as a call to action for national unity and defense of democratic principles. The *New York Times* noted Biden's focus on threats to democracy stemming from the actions of Trump and "MAGA forces." Similarly, *POLITICO* described the address as Biden's attempt to frame the upcoming midterm elections as a choice between democracy and the extremism he attributed to MAGA Republicans. *The Washington Post* provided a historical context, noting that this location, where the Declaration of Independence was debated and signed, added weight to Biden's message about safeguarding democracy.

The AP reported that Biden sounded a newly strong alarm about Trumpism's menacing democracy, marking a shift from his earlier calls for unity to a more direct confrontation with what he sees as extremist threats. The BBC described the setting as picturesque with a "dark twist," suggesting that the visuals and the speech's content were intentionally aligned to convey urgency.

Inflation lies

The aforementioned "American Rescue Plan Act" served to explode inflation in America just at the time the economy was starting to naturally recover from the pandemic shut-downs. Employment was ramping up and businesses were re-opening. The $1.9 trillion dollar government bail-out only served to continue the incentives for people to stay unemployed and by injecting so much government money into the economy, the value of the dollar was diminished, thus spiking inflation.

But, Biden wanted to be seen as "doing something" and "taking charge" so without a single Republican vote in Congress and with two Democrats defecting in the House, Biden got to put his signature on stimulus checks and claim he had "done something." He did something all right, he ruined the economy with historic inflation. The average rate of inflation in 2023 was 1.2%. After Biden's first year, it rose to 4.7%. In 2022, the average rate of inflation exploded to 8.0%. In 2023 the average rate of inflation was 4.1%. June of 2022 had the inflation rate topping off at 9.1% year-over-year.

It was a disaster.

When asked about inflation, the Biden Administration spent years denying it was even happening. President Biden falsely claimed that inflation was at 9% when he took office in January 2021. The actual inflation rate at that time was 1.4%, and it did not reach 9% until June 2022, 17 months into his presidency. This claim was made during interviews with CNN and Yahoo Finance in May 2024.

Following the Russian invasion of Ukraine in February 2022, Biden and his administration explicitly linked the spike in inflation, especially gas prices, to "Putin's price hike." Statements from the White House and Biden himself often referred to the invasion as a significant contributor to the inflation surge, particularly for energy prices. This was evident in various official communications and press briefings where the term "#PutinPriceHike" was coined.

It was all a lie.

From claiming there was no inflation, to then claiming inflation was transitory, to then blaming Putin for inflation, to then blaming Trump for inflation, to then falsely claiming they had beaten inflation - Biden and his administration caused record-high inflation and then lied throughout his presidency about it.

Afghanistan withdrawal

Biden first claimed he inherited a doomed plan for withdrawal from Afghanistan from Trump, despite the fact that he supported the plan to withdraw troops while he was running against Trump. Biden promised during his campaign to end the "forever wars," specifically mentioning Afghanistan. He advocated for bringing U.S. troops home. This was framed within the context of ensuring that the withdrawal would not lead to Afghanistan becoming a safe haven for terrorists again, which was precisely Trump's plan as well.

By Spring of 2021, Biden claimed that he had fixed and improved Trump's withdrawal schedule which had targeted May 1, 2021. Biden announced a full withdrawal of U.S. troops from Afghanistan, would instead *commence* on the May 1st date, setting a deadline for September 11, 2021, later adjusted to August 31, 2021. As the withdrawal moved forward, Taliban forces were quickly gaining ground against the Afghan Army and by July it was clear that if the American withdrawal continued apace, the Taliban would dominate and sweep into power.

In a July 8, 2021, Press Conference President Biden provided an update on the situation in Afghanistan and reiterated his commitment to his plan and its effectiveness. He stressed that the withdrawal was proceeding in a secure and orderly manner, with advice from military commanders that speed was key to safety. He also reiterated that the U.S. would maintain the capability to address future terrorist threats from Afghanistan without a permanent troop presence. He emphasized that the future of Afghanistan was for the Afghan people to decide, not the U.S. He stated that Afghan forces had the capacity to defend against the Taliban but questioned their willingness to do so.

Biden mentioned that the U.S. would continue to support Afghan forces and work on peace solutions. He expressed skepticism about a unified government but hoped for some form of power-sharing agreement with the Taliban. When asked specifically about certain parallels between how his troop withdrawal plan had begun to look like America's withdrawal from Vietnam, he was unequivocal. Biden explicitly stated, "There's going to be no circumstance where you see people being lifted off the roof of an embassy of the United States from Afghanistan. It is not at all comparable." He emphasized that the Taliban was not equivalent to the North Vietnamese Army in terms of capability.

Several weeks later, all hell broke loose and the entire world saw images of transport helicopters lifting personnel off the roof of the American embassy.

A brief timeline:

August 14, 2021: The Taliban entered Kabul as Afghan President Ashraf Ghani fled the country, leading to the collapse of the Afghan government. This prompted the U.S. to initiate a massive evacuation operation.

August 15, 2021: Kabul fell to the Taliban. The U.S. Embassy was evacuated, and the American flag was lowered.

The U.S. military took control of Hamid Karzai International Airport (HKIA) to facilitate evacuations.

August 16, 2021: President Biden addressed the nation, defending his decision to withdraw and attributing the rapid collapse to Afghan forces not fighting for their country.

August 26, 2021: A devastating suicide bombing attack by ISIS-K at the Abbey Gate of HKIA killed 13 U.S. service members and at least 170 Afghan civilians. This event was one of the deadliest attacks on U.S. forces in Afghanistan in years.

August 27, 2021: In retaliation, the U.S. military conducted a drone strike aimed at ISIS-K operatives. However, this strike was later acknowledged as a tragic mistake, killing 10 civilians, including seven children.

August 30, 2021: The last U.S. military flight left Afghanistan, marking the official end of the U.S. combat mission which had started in 2001. General Kenneth McKenzie announced the completion of the withdrawal from the Pentagon.

The Afghan withdrawal was an unmitigated disaster with 13 American troops killed and thousands of Afghan allies left behind and in the hands of the Taliban. Biden claimed it was an unmitigated success.

White House Press Secretary Jen Psaki began the lies and they were quickly repeated by other members of the administration and further echoed by the media propagandists. The media highlighted the scale of the evacuation operation, claiming it was one of the largest airlifts in history. Over 120,000 people, including Americans and Afghan allies, were evacuated in a short period. President Biden called this "the extraordinary success of this mission," focusing on the number of people rescued and the complexity of the operation. At the dignified transfer of the remains of the fallen service members, Biden was seen checking his watch, as if he was bored and had somewhere else to go. Psaki subsequently lied in her post-White House book and claimed the watch-checking incident never happened.

For Team Biden, this was the definition of success. The media appeared to concur with their complicit silence and implicit approval of this disaster.

Border Security

President Joe Biden entered the White House on January 20, 2021, and immediately upended every policy Trump had put in place at the Southern Border.

Halt on Border Wall Construction: The President signed an executive order to pause the construction of the border wall along the U.S.-Mexico border, ending the national emergency declaration that Trump used to secure funding for the wall. He claimed this was part of a broader move to redirect funding and reassess the legalities of existing contracts.

End of Remain in Mexico Policy: Biden suspended the Migrant Protection Protocols (MPP), commonly known as the "Remain in Mexico" policy, which required asylum-seekers to wait in Mexico for their U.S. court hearings. Though the policy was officially terminated by the Department of Homeland Security (DHS) in June 2021, legal challenges from a Trump-appointed judge in Texas forced a temporary reinstatement, which was later ended.

Reversal of Asylum Bans: Biden's administration initially kept the Title 42 policy, which allowed for the expulsion of migrants on public health grounds during the COVID-19 pandemic. However, this was ended in May 2023 once the health emergency was over. In its place, the administration implemented new policies aimed at encouraging legal pathways and penalizing illegal crossings which were completely ineffective.

Review of Asylum Processing: Biden ordered a review of the asylum system, focusing on undoing Trump's restrictions like the so-called "transit ban," which required asylum-seekers to apply for protection in countries they transited through before arriving at the U.S. border.

End of Family Separations: Biden established a task force to reunite families separated under Trump's "zero tolerance" policy. This was part of his campaign promise to address the "moral and national shame" of the previous administration's approach.

Deportation Priorities: Biden rescinded Trump's expansive deportation policies, focusing enforcement on national security threats, recent border crossers, and those with convictions for certain crimes, thereby narrowing the scope of who would be prioritized for deportation.

Reversal of Public Charge Rule: The administration reviewed and worked towards reversing Trump's "public charge" rule, which had made it harder for illegal immigrants to gain legal status if they were likely to rely on public benefits.

The results? Absolute disaster.

Since Biden took office, there has been a dramatic and historic increase in encounters at the U.S.-Mexico border, with numbers reaching unprecedented levels. In fiscal year 2023, there were approximately 3.2 million encounters, significantly higher than previous years. The use of the "CBP One" app for scheduling border appointments and the expansion of parole programs for migrants from specific countries (like Venezuela) have been disastrous. These policies acted as a magnet for illegal immigration by providing a perceived legal pathway for entry without sufficient vetting or enforcement. Biden's border team effectively turned illegal immigration into a systematic process leaving the illegal alien with the false perception that the entire entry process was approved and legal.

The administration also reduced interior enforcement, leading to a significant number of illegals being released into the U.S. without immediate deportation or removal proceedings. According to a House Judiciary Committee report, only a small fraction of illegal aliens encountered at the border were placed into proceedings for asylum screening, and even fewer were removed. There have been widespread reports of thousands of unaccompanied minors being lost by the system after being placed with sponsors in the U.S., raising concerns about human trafficking and child welfare. This situation was highlighted as a consequence of weakened vetting processes for sponsors.

The surge in illegal immigration has been directly linked to increased security issues, including the rise of criminal organizations like the Tren de Aragua gang from Venezuela, which was not a significant issue in the U.S. before this administration. This was the direct result of Biden's catch-and-release practices at the border. All the while, Biden, his "Border Czar" Kamala Harris, his Secretary of Homeland Security Alejandro Mayorkas, and his Press Secretaries Psaki and Karine Jean-Pierre all maintained, with straight faces, that the border was secure and there was no crisis there... Until they were forced to admit to the chaos for political purposes

Joe Biden: In January 2023, Biden described the process at the border as "safe and orderly and humane," suggesting security and control over border operations. In June 2024, Biden announced new actions to secure the border, implying acknowledgment of prior security but also a need for further measures.

Kamala Harris: Harris consistently maintained that the border is secure. During a visit to El Paso in June 2021, she emphasized that the administration's immigration system is "orderly and humane," which indirectly suggests security. In a June 2021 press conference, she explicitly stated, "We have a secure border." During her ill-fated campaign for president, Harris promised to secure the border... the border she originally claimed was secure.

Alejandro Mayorkas: Mayorkas repeatedly claimed the border was secure in various contexts: In September 2021, he described the border situation as managed and secure despite "challenges." In November 2022, at a House Committee hearing, Mayorkas maintained that the border was secure when questioned by Republican Representative Dan Bishop. He stated, "Yes, and we are working day in and day out to enhance security, Congressman."

In April 2023, during his testimony to the House Homeland Security Committee, Mayorkas reiterated his claim that the southern border was secure despite being challenged by data points showing surges in illegal immigration, drug seizures, and other apprehensions. He specifically responded to questions about whether he stood by his statement that the border was secure with, "It is my testimony that the border is secure, and we are working every day and night to increase its security." In December 2024, one month after the presidential election, Mayorkas was conceded that the administration could have executed earlier executive actions to secure the border, suggesting in hindsight that there could have been more done if not for "irresponsible politics."

Of course, all the false claims and lies about the border were met with pure, unskeptical credulity from the fourth estate protectors of truth in the legacy media. We had no investigations into the Biden border policies and no fact-checking segments on the Administration's public statements. No scrutiny of missing children or crimes at the hands of unvetted criminal illegals. We experienced no prime-time specials on the plight of victims raped or exploited on the harrowing trek through dangerous terrain and across the border. No border patrol agents were granted anonymity to tell their tales of the incompetent administration and the women and children who were suffering as a result of the broken policies. The media didn't spend any of their precious resources following through on crime reports in major cities where the victims, more often than not, were members of immigrant communities who were terrorized by the illegals welcomed in by Biden and his gang.

In fact, this was the media's full abdication of all of the disasters detailed in this chapter throughout the four years of Biden's presidency. They simply looked the other way. Or, even worse, had features pretending to make the case for the Biden presidency's great and historic successes.

This chapter detailing the monumental and historic catastrophes of the Biden presidency could go on even longer and, frankly could be its own book. We haven't even touched on the debacle over the supply chain, the transportation department disasters, or the DEI programs instituted at the Pentagon resulting in a historic recruitment crisis. We don't have space in this book to explore the politicization of the Justice Department and the Biden Administration's coordination of criminal investigations into his political foes, including President Donald Trump.

We haven't delved into the lies surrounding the president's corrupt son and how President Biden lied all through the campaign, through his presidency, and right up until his final weeks in office when he granted an unprecedented, full pardon covering a decade of crimes Hunter Biden committed on his family's behalf. Nor did the legacy corporate media spend much time exploring these topics either. They had no interest in revealing the truth. Rather, if these issues were discussed at all, it was in the guise of fraudulent "fact-checks" attempting to run interference on behalf of Biden against charges made by Republicans or right-of-center media outlets interested in the obvious, newsworthy stories staring them in the face.

It was a complete and total surrender to the truth and to the basics of political journalism. It will forever be the darkest and saddest era of American political journalism. And it was all to serve their openly stated goal: To stop Donald Trump.

Chapter Five - Cheap Fakes and the Biden Decline

The 46th President of the United States, Joseph Robinette Biden, was mentally and cognitively incapable of carrying out the duties of his office from day 1 of his presidency.

It's a bold assertion that will be disputed and challenged by members of Biden's Administration and by members of the political press. Yet, we have no reason to believe any of them because the White House, the president's cabinet, and the vast majority of the political media lied about and covered up the true nature of Biden's rapid decline until they just couldn't lie about it anymore.

It truly is the greatest political scandal in American history.

For the entire 2020 presidential campaign, Biden was protected by his campaign apparatus and by the very reporters charged with the duty of covering his campaign. In reality, instead of *covering* his campaign, they *covered up for* his campaign. Under the guise of COVID pandemic restrictions, Biden was permitted, without any level of scrutiny, to campaign from the basement of his Delaware home. He conducted Zoom appearances and media hits from his home video installation. He rarely emerged from his home and refused to engage in traditional campaign rallies so he wouldn't suffer comparisons with Trump - who flew across the country holding large, boisterous rallies.

Legacy media rarely commented on Biden's hibernation strategy and never drew the obvious comparison between the somnambulant Biden and the energized Trump. The only commentary they'd make was mostly in condemnation of Trump for his "dangerous" large-capacity gatherings during the pandemic as potential "super-spreader events," never following up on the fact that the rallies didn't actually lead to higher levels of COVID infections in the locations they occurred. The ongoing debates over whether Trump's rallies *correlated* with increased COVID infections versus whether they *caused* increased COVID infections will never truly be resolved, it should be noted that this debate was never even initiated over the ubiquitous and often violent "Black Lives Matter" protests in major American cities the same summer.

Regardless, the American people were never really permitted to judge Biden's competence in an apples-to-apples way since the bulk of Biden's campaigning was performed in a vacuum-sealed video-only bubble, free of any crowds or interactions with the public. It would've been in these types of settings where Biden's true decline could've been witnessed early on. Once inaugurated, Biden was cloistered even more. He rarely gave press conferences and when he did, they were highly scripted and choreographed affairs.

With one exception.

During a White House press conference in January 2022, Newsmax reporter James Rosen asked President Joe Biden about his mental fitness, referencing a recent poll by *Politico*/Morning Consult which indicated that 49% of registered voters disagreed with the statement that "Joe Biden is mentally fit." Biden responded to this question with a humorous quip, saying, "Well, you'll make the judgment whether they're correct," and then moved on without providing in-depth commentary on the concerns about his cognitive abilities. Rosen's follow-up was to inquire why such a large portion of the American electorate held these concerns, to which Biden simply replied, "I have no idea."

Here's the transcript:

JAMES ROSEN, NEWSMAX: Thank you very much for this honor. James Rosen with Newsmax. I'd like to — I'd like to raise a delicate subject but with utmost respect for your life accomplishments and the high office you hold: A poll released, this morning, by Politico/Morning Consult found 49 percent of registered voters disagreeing with the statement, "Joe Biden is mentally fit."

PRESIDENT JOE BIDEN: (Laughs.) Well —

ROSEN: Not even a majority of Democrats who responded strongly affirmed that statement.

BIDEN: Well, I'll let you all make the judgment whether they're correct. Thank you.

ROSEN: Well, so, the question I have for you, sir, before — if you'd let me finish — is: Why do you suppose such large segments of the American electorate have come to harbor such profound concerns about your cognitive fitness? Thank you.

BIDEN: I have no idea.

Rosen, as anyone can see, was overly deferential and polite in asking the question. He acknowledged that it was a delicate subject and he used as the framing of the inquiry a poll from a mainstream publication that had hit just that very morning. Frankly, the most remarkable aspect of the exchange is that it came roughly one hour into the press conference and that no one else from the media bothered to ask such an obvious question.

The fallout of this exchange? Rosen claims he was basically blackballed from full participation in White House briefings for over a year. He would sit for hours without being called upon. Sometimes, he would shout a question and the result was ridicule and condescension, but never an answer to his question.

In January of 2024, Rosen detailed one of his recent exchanges with White House Press Secretary Karine Jean-Pierre on his X account:

After an hour of being ignored at yesterday's White House briefing, I cheerfully shouted out at (Jean-Pierre) to get her to call on me. Jean-Pierre) laughed and declared from the podium: "I love you so much, James." What didn't happen? Me getting called on.

Not one member of the White House Press Corps ever spoke up in Rosen's defense or ever deferred one of their questions to their colleague. Until the middle of 2024, none of them ever bothered to follow up on Rosen's line of questioning in any significant way. It just never occurred to them that Biden was showing signs of mental decline or physical ineptitude. They just didn't see it. They didn't see what every American plainly saw. Which, of course, is absurd.

They saw it. They saw it closer and plainer than any of the rest of us saw it. They had, after all, a front-row seat. They just chose to willfully ignore it. Worse, they chose to lie about it and cast aspersions on the handful of honest, right-of-center journalists who pointed out what everyone on the planet could plainly see. The moment any cracks in the "Joe is perfectly fine" narrative began to show, they'd all work together to patch things up and attack the one or two voices who were daring to step out from the crowd and tell the truth.

The first crack came in the form of a report from US Attorney and Special Counsel Robert Hur who was looking into Biden's mishandling of classified documents that had been discovered in one of his post-Vice Presidency offices as well as the garage of his home in Delaware.

Hur's investigation into Biden's handling of classified documents began in January 2023, when Attorney General Merrick Garland appointed him as special counsel. The investigation concluded in February 2024, with Hur submitting his report to the Justice Department. Despite finding evidence of willful retention, Hur decided not to recommend criminal charges against Biden. This decision was based on the evidence not establishing Biden's guilt beyond a reasonable doubt. Hur noted that prosecuting Biden would be "unwarranted based on our consideration of the aggravating and mitigating factors" outlined in Justice Department policies.

A significant part of Hur's rationale for not charging Biden was related to the President's memory. Hur described Biden as appearing to jurors as, "a sympathetic, well-meaning, elderly man with a poor memory," which would make it difficult to prove willfulness beyond a reasonable doubt. This assessment was based on Biden's interviews where he struggled to recall when his term as vice president ended or when his son Beau died.

The report was devastating. It painted Biden as incapable of recalling basic life events and unable to conduct a thorough recitation of pertinent details in his life. These would be basic abilities that most Americans would want in their doctor, lawyer, or accountant, let alone their president. The media digested this blockbuster story and immediately regurgitated it in the form of an attack on Robert Hur.

Mainstream outlets heavily criticized Hur for describing Biden as, "a sympathetic, well-meaning, elderly man with a poor memory" in his report. This characterization was characterized by Democrats and liberal media, as both politically motivated and unnecessarily harsh. For instance, CNN described these remarks as, "personal and painful jabs at Joe Biden" that went too far beyond the scope of legal analysis required for his report. The Guardian dutifully reported without any challenge or scrutiny that Hur's comments were perceived as "inaccurate and inappropriate" by Vice President Kamala Harris.

There was a narrative pushed by some media outlets and Democratic figures that Hur's report was politically motivated because he is a registered Republican, previously appointed by Donald Trump. The *New York Times* and *The Washington Post*, among others, claimed Hur was trying to influence the election by including the remarks about Biden's mental state. This led to accusations of Hur being a partisan figure rather than an impartial legal investigator.

Media coverage often juxtaposed Hur's findings on Biden with the ongoing legal issues surrounding Donald Trump's handling of classified documents. *The Washington Post* and NBC News, for example, contrasted Biden's so-called cooperation with the investigation against Trump's alleged obstruction. All of these reports attacking Hur somehow ignored the significant evidence found in the report that although Biden had violated the law, the charges wouldn't stick because he didn't have the mental capacity to understand that he had broken the law.

The next crack came in the form of a Wall Street Journal article from spring 2024, titled "Behind Closed Doors, Biden Shows Signs of Slipping." It detailed further concerns about Biden's mental acuity. The piece was based on interviews with over 45 people, including politicians and administration officials. Participants in private meetings with Biden described him as showing signs of cognitive decline, such as speaking softly, relying heavily on notes for policy discussions, and sometimes appearing disengaged or struggling with recall.

The White House and congressional Democrats, staunchly defended Biden, asserting that he was "sharp as a tack" and dismissing any criticism as partisan politics. However, the report highlighted that most of those who expressed concern were Republicans, with some Democrats also acknowledging signs of aging or cognitive decline in private. The article contrasted Biden's public image, where he was often seen with aides guiding him or using teleprompters, with the more concerning observations from closed-door meetings. It noted instances where Biden seemed to depend on others to steer conversations or was observed with "lengthy pauses" or "closing his eyes" during discussions.

Naturally, the media attacked The Wall Street Journal.

CNN labeled the WSJ piece as suffering from "glaring problems" due to its heavy reliance on Republican sources, after all, Republicans can't be trusted on an issue like this. They claimed (without evidence) that the story was part of a GOP-propelled narrative questioning Biden's fitness for office. CNN highlighted the lack of on-the-record comments from Democrats, specifically mentioning that former House Speaker Nancy Pelosi was not quoted despite speaking to the WSJ.

Poynter questioned the veracity of the WSJ story, suggesting it was built on quotes from those with political motives against Biden's reelection. They pointed out that the "money quote" came from Kevin McCarthy, whose statements were inconsistent with his previous remarks about Biden. *Morning Joe* on MSNBC, with host Joe Scarborough, described the WSJ's report as a "Trump hit piece." Scarborough challenged the narrative by referencing other reports where McCarthy had described Biden positively in meetings. He also criticized the WSJ for not quoting high-ranking Democrats who had spoken about Biden's sharpness, despite their willingness to go on record.

With scripted unanimity, a chorus of Democrats and media figures from Kamala Harris to Washington Post columnist Eugene Robinson to actor/activist Michael Douglas all emerged within days of the WSJ article to describe Biden in the exact, same way: "He is sharp as a tack" they all claimed in unison. And, uncannily, his "sharp as a tack" abilities were exclusively on full display behind closed doors, in private meetings.

And, of course, the legacy propagandist media picked up the narrative and repeated it as if it were Gospel truth.

The final cracks in the fake facade came with a series of videos of Biden appearing at multiple high-profile public events in early June of 2024. At these events, his behavior could be directly compared to many people on the same screen with him. Seeing his halting behaviors in these settings made Biden's rapid decline even more obvious and raised alarms across the board.

During his participation at the 80th anniversary of the D-Day invasion, on June 6, 2024, he appeared disoriented. At one point he froze in a half-squat as he was attempting to sit down in a chair. He was seen turning in the opposite direction of the assembled world leaders who were on stage watching a ceremony. As the ceremony ended, rather than stay and greet veterans and other participants, he was seen being rapidly escorted off the stage and out of the event by First Lady Jill Biden.

Later that week, on June 10th, Biden participated in a White House event held in honor of Juneteenth, a holiday commemorating the end of slavery in the United States. The celebration included speeches, and musical performances, and was attended by various public figures, including Vice President Kamala Harris, Philonise Floyd (brother of George Floyd), and other notable guests. During a musical performance, specifically when gospel singer Kirk Franklin was performing, Biden, who was standing with others on stage, seemed to pause or freeze for several seconds. His gaze was fixed, and he appeared less responsive than those around him, who were clapping and engaging with the performance.

His facial expression (or lack thereof) appeared exactly as it had during the more disconcerting moments at the D-Day commemoration. Video of the moment, like video of the D-Day event, took off on social media raising further concerns over the president's health and ability.

Several days later, Biden was back in Europe. This time attending the G7 summit in Italy. During a skydiving demonstration attended by the leaders of the world's seven largest economies, (not including China and India) which included Canada, France, Germany, Italy, Japan, and the United Kingdom, Biden (naturally representing the USA) appeared to wander away from his six counterparts who were all attentively observing the paratroopers landing in front of them. The President moved away from the group to give a thumbs-up to one of the parachutists and a parachute rigger who was kneeling on the ground behind the group. Italian Prime Minister Giorgia Meloni then gently guided him back to the group where an Italian Army officer was briefing the leaders. The video clearly showed Biden going off on his own and not understanding what he and the other leaders were doing and where his attention was supposed to be. Meloni's deft and diplomatic maneuver telegraphed that she and the others knew that Biden was in need of some guidance.

Like the other two videos, the G7 clip was widely shared on social media and streaming platforms. The obvious reaction (coupled with the Juneteenth and D-Day videos) was of grave concern over the current mental state of the leader of the free world. Three videos in June that all told the same story. The oldest president in American history, who was currently running for re-election, was seriously debilitated.

And it was only June 13th - we still had one more video to go.

At a June 15th presidential fundraiser at the Peacock Theatre in Los Angeles, Biden appeared to, once again, freeze on stage. This time, he was with former President Barack Obama, and talk show host Jimmy Kimmel. Video footage from the event showed Biden and Obama standing to receive applause after a sit-down interview with Kimmel. Biden appeared to pause, staring out at the audience for about seven seconds before Obama gently guided him off stage.

The moment may have gone without much commentary or analysis, but after the prior three videos over the course of just nine days, this final "senior moment" finally led to serious questions from reporters in the White House briefing room. Even they couldn't ignore this any longer. Finally, James Rosen had some company.

Well, sort of.

At a press briefing on June 17th, Associated Press National P{political Reporter Will Weissert seemed to suggest that the rash of videos had been edited in some sort of deceptive way. Jean-Pierre had a prepared response set up on one of her briefing book plastic tabs. She turned to it and let loose on what she called "cheap fake" videos.

WEISSERT: There seems to be a sort of a rash of videos that have been edited to make the president appear officially frail or mentally confused. I'm wondering if the White House is especially worried about the fact that this appears to be a pattern.

KARINE JEAN-PIERRE: Yeah, and I think you all have called this the "cheap fakes" video and that's exactly what they are. They are cheap fake videos, they are done in bad faith and, and some of your news organizations have been very clear, have stressed that these right-wing, the right-wing critics of the president have a credibility problem because of the fact-checkers have repeatedly caught them pushing misinformation, disinformation.

And so we see this and this is something coming from your part of the world, calling them cheap fakes and misinformation. And I'll quote The Washington Post where they wrote, they wrote about this and they said how "Republicans used misleading videos to attack Biden in a 24-hour period" and to their credit, we have a conservative Washington Examiner did call them out as well, calling out the New York Post.

Ironically several recent cheap fakes actually attack the president for thanking troops -- for thanking troops. That is what they're attacking the president for, both in Normandy this happened and again in Italy, and I think that it tells you everything that we need to know about how, how desperate, how desperate Republicans are here. And instead of talking about the president's performance in office, and what I mean by that is his legislative wins, what he's been able to do for the American people across the country, we're seeing these deepfakes, these manipulated videos. And it is again done in bad faith.

Amazing.

You see what she did there, right?

First, she consistently referenced the helpful, partisan, propaganda media outlets as if they were some sort of unbiased arbiters of truth on this topic. "I'll quote *The Washington Post* where they wrote..." and, "I think you all have called this the "cheap fakes" video and that's exactly what they are..." Most people have heard of "Deep Fake" videos that utilize CGI and Artificial Intelligence to produce fraudulent, yet very realistic" videos of famous people. Deepfakes are incredibly realistic, but can usually be discerned from an authentic video of the individuals depicted.

"Cheap fake" videos, on the other hand... What the heck are they? And why is Jean-Pierre referencing them as if they were some sort of common thing? The term "cheap fakes" was coined in 2019 by Britt Paris and Joan Donovan, co-authors of "Deep Fakes *and Cheap Fakes: The Manipulation of Audio and Visual Evidence.*" They defined it as an audiovisual (AV) manipulation created with cheaper, more accessible software, or even without any software at all, as opposed to deepfakes which involve more sophisticated AI technology.

The White House was prepared for questions about the growing concerns over the videos showing Biden frail, lost and frozen so they researched an answer that would blame the messengers rather than recognize the obvious truth that Biden was debilitated. They found the "cheap fake" narrative and planted it, deliberately, at the press briefing. On June 17th, the same day as Jean-Pierre's "Cheap Fake" narrative, NBC News published an article titled "Misleading GOP videos of Biden are going viral. The fact-checks have trouble keeping up."

The article, by Senior Political Reporter Alex Seitz-Wald, claimed the string of videos of Biden had all been manipulated in some rudimentary way and presented to make Biden appear infirmed or out of it, even though he was, what's the phrase? "Sharp as a TACK!"

The propaganda piece included this gem:

At the fundraiser in Los Angeles, Biden and Obama were waving to supporters after having received a standing ovation when Biden stared into the audience for a moment before the more punctual Obama signaled it was time to leave the stage. Several people at the event said they did not recognize the New York Post's interpretation that Biden appeared to "freeze up."

Oh my. Biden stared into the audience "for a moment" compared to the "more punctual" Obama. That's just precious. How long is "a moment" Mr. Seitz-Wald? And was Obama merely being "more punctual" by exiting the stage in a timely manner? Was that *really* all that was at play here? Or, could the exact same video also be described as Biden, "staring into the timeless void for over five seconds until Obama, recognizing he was frozen and lost, grabbed his wrist and shook him back to reality"?

Yes, it could very easily be described that way. But Alex Seitz-Wald had taken it upon himself to declare what the truth was in this case. And, shockingly, the truth favored Biden and the White House narrative. He concluded with:

Taking liberties with video editing — or simply misrepresenting what is happening in a video — is nothing new. But former President Donald Trump's takeover of the Republican Party has pushed the party further across the hazy divide between spin and mendacity, while technology has allowed for clips to be cut and broadcast constantly.

CBS News took on the job of explaining the "Cheap fake" narrative to their viewers on June 19th.

Misleading video clips of President Biden watching a skydiving demonstration at the G7 summit in Italy went viral last week, prompting the White House to say Biden is victim to a simpler version of "deepfakes." So, what are "cheap fakes"?

Of course, the answer to CBS News' question was pretty much exactly what the White House had said two days earlier at the briefing. The Associated Press's June 21st article was headlined, "Seeing is believing? Not necessarily when it comes to video clips of Biden and Trump."

The "Cheap fake" defense crafted at the White House seemed to have worked. The legacy propagandists at the corporate outlets had effectively accused right-of-center outlets of taking manipulated videos from the Trump campaign and creating a false narrative that Biden had "lost it." The strategy had the dual effect of deflecting the very real concerns that the majority of Americans were feeling about Biden and simultaneously accusing Trump and his pals in the right-wing media of lying and manipulating the American people.

They would have gotten away with their "cheap fake" lies if it hadn't been for the presidential debate between Biden and Trump that took place on June 27th.

When Joe Biden took the stage that fateful evening, just 21 days after the first video from Normandy began circulating and just ten days after corporate media propagandists took the "cheap fakes" distortion from the White House and turned it into DC conventional wisdom, he could no longer hide the obvious and devastating decline he had suffered over the past several years. For 90 minutes he struggled, he stammered, he got lost in thought, and he could barely even be heard on his microphone as he tried to match wits with Donald Trump. At the end of those 90 minutes, not only were the moderators, CNN's Jake Tapper and Dana Bash admitting the obvious, but so were the rest of the media hacks who had ignored, lied, and covered up what every American knew.

Joe Biden's hopes for a second term were officially over, it just took the President's team a couple more weeks to fully acknowledge that reality. When they did, an extraordinary and unprecedented bloodless coup was engineered behind the scenes installing Vice President Kamala Harris as the new nominee for President without a single vote. But what about the shameless liars in the legacy media standing guard against the powerful elite, looking out for the average American voter? Oh, they were just fine with the whole theatrical farce.

In fact, they were co-stars and co-authors of the whole outrageous fiction.

Chapter Six - Biden Falls And Can't Get Up

The political earthquake that reverberated through the United States the evening of June 27th was catastrophic for President Biden, the Democrats, and the media propagandists who had been propping up the octogenarian President from Delaware since the campaign of 2020. Social media reaction from journalists was stunning. After years of covering up the obvious decline - and just days after accusing right-of-center media figures of misinformation as we detailed in the previous chapter - these same reporters, analysts, and hosts couldn't deny the truth.

Joy Reid (MSNBC): Described Biden's performance as "extremely feeble and weak," reflecting a sense of panic among party figures. She noted that her phone was buzzing with texts from people in Obamaworld and Bidenworld, indicating widespread concern within the party.

Van Jones (CNN): "I love Joe Biden. But tonight's debate hurt," and he described the reaction among supporters as not just panic but pain, suggesting Biden failed a crucial test to restore the country's confidence in his capabilities.

Joe Scarborough (MSNBC): On *Morning Joe*, Scarborough admitted his love for Biden but criticized his debate performance by rhetorically asking if Biden would be retained as CEO of a corporation after such a showing, highlighting the performance's implications on Biden's candidacy for reelection.

David Axelrod (CNN): Axelrod, a former advisor to President Obama, noted that Biden's performance "confirmed people's fears" about his age, signaling that it was a significant setback for Biden's campaign. He was among those who suggested that the debate had validated concerns about Biden's mental acuity.

Kate Bedingfield (CNN): Biden's former 2020 campaign manager, appearing on CNN, acknowledged there was no way to interpret Biden's debate performance as good, further fueling discussions on Biden's fitness for another term.

Nicholas Kristof (The *New York Times*): Kristof called for Biden to consider stepping down from the race, suggesting that figures like Michigan Governor Gretchen Whitmer or Commerce Secretary Gina Raimondo could be better positioned to defeat Trump. This reflected a broader sentiment among some Democrats post-debate.

Biden's lamentable performance was even worse considering he had spent the entire week preceding the showdown in Atlanta at the Camp David presidential retreat to engage in intense preparation. Despite the "murder boards" and mock debates with his team of trainers and tutors, the President of the United States seemed clueless.

Lost in Biden's awful debate performance was the reality that it was actually Trump's finest debate since the 2016 primaries. He was magnificent and controlled and disciplined and engaged. Biden's horrible performance appeared that much worse because it was compared side-by-side with Trump's brilliant debate performance.

It was devastating for the Democratic Party incumbent. Something had to be done!

Vice President Kamala Harris was dispatched to CNN's Anderson Cooper Tonight to spin Biden's performance immediately after the debate and it did not go well for the Gentlewoman from California.

ANDERSON COOPER: CNN's John King has described a panic inside the Democratic Party right now because of President Biden's performance in tonight's debate. He's been hearing from Democratic lawmakers and others around the country. Some within your own party are wondering if President Biden should even step aside. What do you say to that?

KAMALA HARRIS: Listen, first of all, what we saw tonight is the president making a very clear contrast with Donald Trump on all of the issues that matter to the American people.

Yes, there was a slow start, but it was a strong finish. And what became very clear through the course of the night is that Joe Biden is fighting on behalf of the American people, on substance, on policy, on performance. Joe Biden is extraordinarily strong and–

COOPER: All that may be true. But the president of the United States was not able to -- to put -- make that case to Donald Trump on the stage tonight. I mean, you debated against then Vice President Trump -- excuse me, Vice President Biden four years ago, and he was a very different person on the stage four years ago when -- when you debated him. You must -- I mean, that -- that's certainly true, is it not?

HARRIS: Anderson, the point has to be performance in terms of what a president does. A president who incites an insurrection against the Capitol --

COOPER: But that is what is scary for people watching this.

HARRIS: But I got the point that you're making about a one-and-a-half-hour debate tonight. I'm talking about three and a half years of performance in work that has been historic, whether that be infrastructure. The former guy, the other guy -- the other guy on the debate stage --

COOPER: But is that the man -- the man who we saw on the stage tonight, is that the person you see --

HARRIS: The person that you saw on the debate stage that has for the last three and a half years, up until today, performed in a way that has been about, whether it be in the Oval Office, negotiating bipartisan deals so that we have an infrastructure, a real infrastructure plan where we're putting trillions of dollars on the streets of America to upgrade our infrastructure, whether it be the person I see in the Oval Office who is meeting with heads of the military and the Intelligence Community and in the Situation Room, ensuring the safety of America, the person I see in Joe Biden on the world stage convening world leaders who often ask for his advice, most recently just during the G7 conference.

So, I'm not going to spend all night with you talking about the last 90 minutes when I've been watching the last three and a half years of performance.

Ouch.

Meanwhile, things got worse for Biden as he and First Lady Jill appeared at a post-debate pep rally populated by supporters. The First Lady stood center stage with the microphone while a feeble and exhausted Biden looked on helplessly.

"Joe, you did such a great job! You answered every question, you knew all the facts!" Jill Biden exclaimed to a grinning Joe Biden on stage.

First Lady Jill Biden is either blessed or plagued (we report, you decide) with an incredibly juvenile-sounding voice. Everything she says on the public stage ends up sounding like she's talking to a room full of Kindergarten children. For some, this quality could be endearing. But, in the context of this post-debate moment, it was a catastrophe. Her sing-song delivery of, "You answered every question," came across as a woman giving over-the-top encouragement to a toddler going through a potty-training exercise. "You made a poo-poo like such a big boy," is not too far from the sound of her praise for her husband who was not only a 50-year veteran of American politics, but was also - let's not forget - the then-current President of the United States. How, exactly, is "answering every question" such a praise-worthy achievement?

The video was so devastating it went nearly as viral on social media as the multiple clips of the actual debate where Biden meandered from forgotten talking point to forgotten talking point in a raspy, barely audible voice.

Within minutes of the conclusion of the debate, it was spun to network anchors by campaign operatives that the President had been suffering from a terrible illness and that was why he was a bit "off his game." Strange, that in the hours of pre-debate coverage from all the networks who were obsessively hyping the event, not one person with direct sources at the Biden campaign ever mentioned Biden had even the slightest sniffle, let alone the full-blown illness they were now suggesting he was suffering from.

Naturally, television hosts, reporters, and commentators all repeated the "Biden is sick" spin as if it were Gospel truth written by St. Mark himself. Incredibly, after the pep rally and while the "Biden is deathly ill" lie was being credulously repeated by our media, the Biden's immediately went to a local Waffle House to mingle with "real people" eating a late-night snack. There was old Joe, shaking hands, hugging and spreading germs at a diner as people were eating, waitresses were serving and cooks were preparing food.

"If he is so sick, why in the hell isn't he in bed recovering, and what in hell is he doing at a restaurant spreading germs around while people are trying to eat?" asked any person with a brain, except members of the legacy media, of course.

But nobody was buying it. The tidal wave was growing bigger and bigger and it just couldn't be stopped. Biden was done, but he and the campaign were in denial.

The immediate strategy to repair the damage done was to get Biden in front of rallies and to have him sit for major media interviews to prove he was just fine. While the candidate was doing that, the media would repeat the assertion that Trump lied his way through the debate. Apparently, the messaging everyone agreed on was, "Biden may have dementia, but Trump lied, so…" Yeah, they didn't really have a conclusion to that sentence because as soon as the "Biden may have dementia" hit home, whatever Trump said really didn't matter. Biden's first media appearance was with the more-than-eager-to-help Democrat operative posing as a network newsman George Stephanopoulos.

"Look, I have a cognitive test every single day," Biden said. "Every day, I've had tests. Everything I do. You know, not only am I campaigning, I'm running the world. And that's not — it sounds like hyperbole, but we are the central nation of the world."

Stephanopoulos asked if he had replayed the debate and watched it and Biden said, "I don't think I did, no."

"I don't think anybody's more qualified to be president or win this race than me," Biden added.

It may be hard to believe, but that exchange did not assuage concerns that Biden wasn't ready for four more years in the highest-pressure job on the planet.

Next came NBC News' Lester Holt.

LESTER HOLT: In your last TV interview you were asked if you had watched the debate and your answer was, "I don't think so, no." Have you since seen it?

PRESIDENT JOE BIDEN: I've seen pieces of it. I've not watched the whole debate.

HOLT: And — and the reason I ask, because I guess the question is are you all on the same page as to where — are you seeing what they saw, which was moments of, frankly, it — it appeared to be you — you appeared to be confused.

BIDEN: Lester, look, why don't you guys ever talk about the 18 — the 28 lies he told? Where — where are you on this? Why doesn't the press ever talk about that? Twenty-eight times, it's confirmed, he lied in that debate. I had a bad, bad night. I wasn't feeling well at all. And — and I had been — without making — I screwed up. But —

HOLT: The re — I just ask the question because — the — the idea that you may or may not have seen what some of these other folks have seen. You're not on the same —

BIDEN: I didn't have to see it — I was there. (LAUGH) I didn't have to see it. I was there. And by the way, seriously, you won't answer the question, but why doesn't the press talk about all the lies he told? I haven't heard —

HOLT: Well, we —

BIDEN: — anything about that.

HOLT: We — we have reported many of the issues that came of that —

BIDEN: No you haven't —

HOLT: — that debate.

BIDEN: No you haven't.

HOLT: Well, we'll provide you with them.

BIDEN: God love you.

It became clear to the American people and even Biden's pals in the media that not only was Biden in no condition to be president through 2028, but he wasn't in any condition to perform the job *today*. Of greater concern to the Democrats and the press, Biden was in no position to run a campaign - let alone the country. And to them, running the country was far less important than defeating Donald Trump. By the first week of July, that notion seemed like a pipe dream.

Something had to be done.

Biden and the Democrats had boxed themselves in with very few options at this point. The party refused to participate in any legitimate primary process in the Spring of 2024. Despite lifelong Democrat Robert F. Kennedy Jr.'s challenge to wrestle the nomination from Biden (reminiscent of his Uncle Teddy's Quixotic primary campaign in 1980 against his party's incumbent, Jimmy Carter) the Democrat establishment was determined to ride Biden to reelection. They convinced themselves that only Biden could beat back a challenge from Trump, so they stacked the deck and rigged the primary process to ensure that Biden would be nominated without anything resembling a legitimate challenge. Kennedy was so disillusioned and, frankly, pissed off, he left the party and started an independent run that eventually turned into an unprecedented endorsement of Trump that could very well have changed the entire dynamic of the election.

It was all due to the arrogance and myopic obsession with protecting Biden from any challenge. Now, after the debate disaster and the failed attempts to clean up the mess, Democrats had few if any options.

It was early July. Their nominating convention was four weeks away. They couldn't, realistically, mount a 50-state primary process to have voters decide a replacement nominee. Not to mention the fact that the current nominee, the incumbent president, still hadn't gotten the message that he was about to be removed from the ticket.

Enter Nancy Pelosi.

The fellow octogenarian who had stood astride the power structure of the Democrat party apparatus for nearly two decades became the sounding board for party power players, donors, and media giants who knew they were doomed with Biden as their nominee. She was hearing it from all sides and she knew, herself, that Biden had to go.

During a media appearance on MSNBC Pelosi gave far less than a full-throated endorsement of her life-long friend and political ally. "It's up to the president to decide if he is going to run. We're all encouraging him to make that decision because time is running short," she said. With friends like these…

Pelosi wasn't alone.

Senate Majority Leader and long-time Biden ally Chuck Schumer (no spring chicken himself at the ripe old age of 74) also gave not-very-veiled indications that it was time for Biden to exit stage-extreme-left.

Schumer had a "blunt" conversation with Biden, making the case that it would be best for Biden, the Democratic Party, and the country if he dropped out of the race. This was reported by ABC News, NBC News, and other outlets, citing multiple sources familiar with the discussion.

On the third Sunday of July, one month after the single worst presidential debate performance in American history, everything was turned upside down.

Chapter Seven - The Kamala Coup

At 1:46 PM ET, on July 21, 2024, the "X" account managed by the Biden campaign issued the following statement:

"My Fellow Americans, Over the past three and a half years, we have made great progress as a Nation. Today, America has the strongest economy in the world. We've made historic investments in rebuilding our Nation, in lowering prescription drug costs for seniors, and in expanding affordable health care to a record number of Americans. We've provided critically needed care to a million veterans

exposed to toxic substances. Passed the first gun safety law in 30 years.

Appointed the first African American woman to the Supreme Court. And passed the most significant climate legislation in the history of the world. America has never been better positioned to lead than we are today.

I know none of this could have been done without you, the American people. Together, we overcame a once in a century pandemic and the worst economic crisis since the Great Depression. We've protected and preserved our Democracy. And we've revitalized and strengthened our alliances around the world.

It has been the greatest honor of my life to serve as your President. And while it has been my intention to seek reelection, I believe it is in the best interest of my party and the country for me to stand down and to focus solely on fulfilling my duties as President for the remainder of my term. I will speak to the Nation later This Week in more detail about my decision.

For now, let me express my deepest gratitude to all those who have worked so hard to see me reelected. I want to thank Vice President Kamala Harris for being an extraordinary partner in all this work. And let me express my heartfelt appreciation to the American people for the faith and trust you have placed in me. I believe today what I always have: that there is nothing America can't do -- when we do it together. We just have to remember we are the United States of America."

All hell immediately broke loose.

The wild speculation, jockeying, and political maneuvering were hitting a fevered pitch. "Will they have a mini-primary?" "Will they have an open convention?" "Will the 'Uncommitted Delegates' stage a coup?" "Will the donors decide?"

Before any of these questions could be answered, (or even asked in some cases) Biden intervened with another extraordinary statement on the X platform.

At 2:46 PM ET, one hour after his withdrawal from the presidential race, Biden named his successor:

"My fellow Democrats, I have decided not to accept the nomination and to focus all my energies on my duties as President for the remainder of my term. My very first decision as the party nominee in 2020 was to pick Kamala Harris as my Vice President. And it's been the best decision I've made. Today I want to offer my full support and endorsement for Kamala to be the nominee of our party this

year. Democrats — it's time to come together and beat Trump. Let's do this."

Despite Biden's endorsement of Harris, Democrat leaders who appeared to be pulling the strings for the entire scenario, attempted to encourage a very different process than Biden's attempted succession plan.

Nancy Pelosi immediately voiced support for an "open nomination process." Reports indicated that in discussions with fellow California Democrats, she stressed the importance of having an open process to choose the party's next nominee, particularly to avoid the appearance of a "Kamala Harris coronation." This was highlighted in various media reports, where Pelosi was noted as advocating for a competitive and inclusive process rather than a quick endorsement of Harris.

Pelosi has subsequently expressed that had Biden dropped out sooner, there could have been an open primary, which might have allowed for more candidates to enter the race and potentially made the process more competitive. She acknowledged that Biden's immediate endorsement of Harris after his exit made an open primary "almost impossible" at that juncture.

Likewise, former President Barack Obama made several comments regarding his vision for a nominating process.

Obama praised Biden's decision to step aside, calling it a "testament to Joe Biden's love of country" and highlighting Biden's character and achievements. However, he notably did not endorse Harris directly. Instead, Obama expressed confidence in the Democratic Party's ability to navigate the "uncharted waters" ahead, stating, "But I have extraordinary confidence that the leaders of our party will be able to create a process from which an outstanding nominee emerges." This was clearly a call for an open convention process rather than an immediate endorsement of Harris.

Neither party elders would see their visions come to fruition.

Kamala Harris was engineering a Machiavellian jiu-jitsu move behind the scenes. Before any of the Democrats who were terrified of the prospect of Biden sticking it out to a humiliating defeat in November could realize what was happening, the Biden campaign swiftly transformed into the Harris campaign. The delegates that had already been pledged to the aging incumbent began pledging their fealty en masse to Madame Vice President.

Within just a few days, the coronation Pelosi feared was inevitable.

Nancy Pelosi endorsed Kamala Harris for president on July 22, the day after Biden's announcement. Former President

Barack Obama officially endorsed Harris for the nomination on July 26, four days after Pelosi. The Kamala Coup was complete.

Enter the propagandists:

The media almost unanimously fell in line with Kamala's candidacy and some even praised her conniving behind the scenes to un-democratically lock up the nomination. They covered the strategic aspects of her nomination, including the decision to hold a virtual vote before the convention due to ballot access laws that required the nomination to be secured prior to the scheduled Democratic convention in August, and the rapid fundraising and endorsements she received, which were seen as signs of strong backing within the party.

Instead of raising their hands and saying "Hey… we're supposed to be Democrats over here. Is anybody else concerned about the whole 'lack of voting by ordinary citizens' thing?" Or, "Um… we've been saying Donald Trump is a 'threat to Democracy' but didn't we just choose our nominee behind closed doors and force her on the American people without the benefit of an election? Isn't *that* kind of a threat to democracy?"

Nope. Nary a peep from the same "journalists" who had spent the past several years warning the country that Trump was an existential threat to Democracy.

Liberal media outlets like NPR, CNN, and The Guardian emphasized the "rapid unification" of the Democrats behind Harris. They highlighted her as the sole candidate to secure the necessary delegate signatures to be on the ballot, portraying this as a "smooth transition" and a "testament to party cohesion." For example, NPR focused on her "historic" potential as the first woman president if elected, while CNN marveled at how she quickly accumulated support from state delegations to meet the nomination threshold.

Some exceptions to the pivot in favor of Harris' historic (if undemocratic) ascendence:

The Intercept: Known for its progressive stance, The Intercept published articles questioning the speed and lack of an open primary after Biden's withdrawal. They highlighted concerns about democratic processes within the party, suggesting that Harris's quick endorsement might have bypassed a more inclusive selection.

Jacobin: The liberal magazine covered the nomination process, focusing on how it seemed to favor establishment candidates over more progressive ones, and criticized the lack of debate or competition in the nomination after Biden's exit.

The Nation: While supportive of progressive causes, The Nation published pieces that critiqued the Democratic Party for not allowing a more open contest. They discussed the implications of a seemingly pre-determined nomination for party unity and voter enthusiasm.

Slate: Although Slate's coverage was mixed, some of its opinion pieces and editorials expressed concern over the process's transparency and inclusivity. Writers pointed out that while unity was important, the method of nomination could have been more democratic.

Mother Jones: This extreme left-wing outlet had commentary on the nomination process, focusing on how the Democratic Party's quick consolidation behind Harris might not have been the best approach for energizing the base or for ensuring the best candidate was chosen.

As one can see, the only criticism of the Kamala Coup came from the far left who were mostly concerned that the candidate chosen by the establishment elders was not sufficiently socialist for their tastes. The establishment media, left-aligned with the establishment party, fell in line and pulled their weight by ignoring altogether the obviously undemocratic putsch. They were just fine with the authoritarian, undemocratic tactics because, as you know, Trump was an undemocratic authoritarian, so, it was ok.

The acquiescence to Harris was a little strange, though, considering up until this very moment, there had been grave concerns over her political prospects. Before the events of the Summer of 2024, Democrat Party leaders and their partners in the corporate media had very strong opinions about the questionable political skills of Vice President Harris. And, mostly, those opinions were not very flattering. Sometimes, these hesitations were spoken out loud.

In an interview for a local Boston radio station in late January, Massachusetts Senator Elizabeth Warren, once a rival for the presidential nomination against both Biden and Harris in 2020, was enthusiastic about President Joe Biden running for reelection. When asked if Biden should keep Harris as his running mate, she said, "I really want to defer to what makes Biden comfortable on his team." Hardly a ringing endorsement. Actually, not in any way an endorsement at all.

Prominent voices in the propaganda media echoed these concerns.

As early as Sept. 13, 2023, New York magazine columnist Eric Levitz penned an article titled, *The Case for Biden to Drop Kamala Harris.*

In it, Levitz revealed in his own voice, what many of his colleagues in the media and in Democrat Party leadership were saying to each other, behind closed doors:

However bad Biden's numbers are, Vice-President Kamala Harris's look worse. A CBS News–YouGov poll released last week found 42 percent of Americans saying that the job Harris is doing makes them think worse of the Biden Administration, compared to just 18 percent who said it makes them feel better about the White House. Among independents, 48 percent said worse and only 9 percent better. Even among Democrats, only 41 percent said Harris made them think better of the administration. At the same time, only 30 percent of Democrats said that they felt "enthusiastic" about Harris being Biden's running mate.

A YouGov poll from May showed 48 percent of Americans said Harris was not ready to assume the presidency, while 32 percent said she was. Again, independents took a dim view, saying 57 to 22 that she wasn't ready. By contrast, in August 2020, 44 percent of voters said that Mike Pence was ready to serve. In FiveThirtyEight's polling average, only 39.5 percent of voters approve of Harris's job performance.

Thus, there is a strong case for Biden to pick a new running mate for 2024, one with a more promising electoral track record and approval rating than Harris. Doing so would plausibly improve his odds of winning next November and put Democrats in a better position come 2028.

But, miraculously, after Harris secured the nomination, Levitz became Harris's biggest fan. Using his X social media account he waxed poetic about how amazing Harris, (the same candidate he "made the case" for dropping less than a year earlier) clearly was:

On her speaking abilities:

Being a good orator is not necessarily the most important thing in politics. But I did not fully appreciate how much better Kamala is at speaking than Whitmer or Shapiro. She is more charismatic than the other imagined Biden alternatives, for whatever that's worth · Aug 22, 2024

On her policy approach:

Harris is taking an unconventional approach to "moderation" -- pivoting right on the border while embracing some very leftwing economic policies (that poll well). There's reason to think that this may be more effective than across-the-board centrism · Aug 19, 2024

Levitz wasn't alone in his new-found adoration for Kamala Harris. It's almost like they all received the same direction. Most analysts who expressed grave concerns about Harris staying on the ticket as Biden's running mate just months earlier were now all-in with the transcendent and game-changing political skills of Harris as the nominee at the top of the ticket.

Strangely, though, the praise for Harris didn't often focus on her legislative achievements as a senator or her incredible record as Attorney General of California. Likewise, the media didn't even *try* to pretend her tenure as Vice President was anything more than a punchline. No, the media praise for Harris seemed to focus almost entirely on, let's call them the "intangibles" of Harris's attributes as the Democrats' nominee for president.

Her race, ethnicity, and her sex.

The coverage often celebrated the historic nature of Harris's candidacy, noting her status as the first Black woman and first South Asian woman to be nominated by a major political party. Though, strangely, the emphasis was very much on the former and not the latter. The emphasis of her African heritage over her Indian heritage was strange because when she became a U.S. Senator the emphasis was almost entirely on her Indian heritage.

Why? Because there had already been a female, African-American senator, but there hadn't been a female, *Indian-American* senator. And the liberal media really do love their "firsts." Her Indian heritage made her a trailblazer when she went to the Senate so that was the emphasis. "Who cares if just another black woman won a senate election?" they seemed to be saying. "We've got to make her a historic figure, somehow, so let's talk about her Indian heritage." They seemed to all agree at the exact same time.

And, naturally, the Harris PR machine was happy to oblige. Looking back at that victory, the overwhelming press coverage focused on her Southeast Asian heritage, almost at the expense of her father's black Jamaican ethnicity. That all changed when she ascended to the 2024 presidential nomination. Now, she was "the first black woman *this*" and "the first black woman *that*." The pivot was obvious and absurd.

There was a modicum of focus on Harris's policy positions and how she would differentiate herself from Biden. The *New York Times*, for instance, explored her stance on various issues like health care, immigration, and social justice, offering insights into her policy pitch to voters as she prepared for the general election against Donald Trump. However, despite her left-of-socialist-Bernie-Sanders record in the Senate and in her failed attempt at winning the 2020 nomination, Harris abandoned her extreme liberal positions almost as soon as the *New York Times* celebrated how "progressive" she'd be compared to Biden. These 180-degree spins continued unabated.

Whatever the media had said about Harris before she became the presumptive nominee was memory-holed and flushed. She was now transcendent and incandescent. She was now the best nominee the Democrats had ever dreamed of having. She was now perfect.

In reality, she was their *only* hope of defeating Trump so they *had* to fall in line. She was all they had, so they worked to convince the American people she was the second coming of President Barack Obama. Strangely, they seemed to be trying to convince *themselves* of this at the same time.

But by the time the end of July was upon them, they had seemingly convinced themselves of their own mythology. They were no longer slow-walking through the muggy days of summer dreading Trump's high-flying poll numbers. They were now in the middle of something called "Brat Summer."

"Brat Summer" was a manufactured viral social media trend and campaign strategy adopted by Harris' presidential campaign the final week of July, almost immediately after Biden announced he would not seek re-election. The trend was sparked by British pop star Charli XCX, who released an album titled "Brat" in June 2024. The album's simple, neon-green cover with "brat" in lowercase became an Internet sensation among teen girls and twenty-something women, symbolizing a lifestyle of being "unapologetically oneself, messy, and confident." Charli XCX endorsed Harris early on X with the tweet "kamala IS brat," which went viral.

Harris's campaign quickly embraced this trend, changing the banner on their official X account to mimic the "Brat" album cover's aesthetic, now reading "kamala hq" on a lime green background. This was part of a broader strategy to engage with younger voters on social media, particularly through platforms like TikTok where "brat summer" videos featuring Harris went viral. The "Brat Summer" for Harris involved leveraging memes, especially those related to her embarrassing gaffe-like quotes like, "You think you just fell out of a coconut tree?" which became part of the "Operation Coconut Tree" meme among her supporters. This was intended to portray Harris as relatable, fun, and engaging, (rather than embarrassing and strange as most *adults* viewed the "coconut tree" moment) aligning with the "brat" ethos of being honest, blunt, and a bit volatile.

Predictably, media outlets like CNN, MSNBC, and The Guardian covered the "Brat Summer" phenomenon, often with a mix of amusement and analysis on how it would influence young voters. In reality, "Brat Summer" was a sign of political desperation and was indicative of the campaign's attempt to trivialize the electoral process and focus on Harris as a "brand" rather than a potential president. The campaign's move was hailed as an "innovative way to connect with Generation Z," leveraging pop culture to make politics more engaging. It aimed to counter perceptions of Harris as stiff or overly serious, presenting a more approachable side.

In an article titled, "'Kamala IS brat': Harris campaign goes lime-green to embrace the meme of the summer," The Guardian highlighted how Harris's campaign "cleverly" adopted the "brat" meme to resonate with younger voters. They noted the cultural impact of Charli XCX's endorsement and the campaign's quick response to it, suggesting it was a smart move to engage with a new demographic. CNN covered the phenomenon with a panel discussion, where Jake Tapper notably said he "will aspire to be brat," indicating the light-hearted and engaging nature of the campaign's strategy. They discussed how this meme could potentially energize young voters, showcasing the campaign's adeptness at tapping into current cultural trends.

The Conversation published an article titled, "How 'brat summer' may be propelling Kamala Harris to the American Presidency." It praised the campaign for recognizing the importance of young voters and committing to meeting them where they are (i.e., on social media) with memes and viral content. The piece analyzed how this could influence voter turnout among the youth.

CBS News published an article titled "How the 'brat summer' TikTok trend kickstarted Kamala Harris campaign memes," praising the campaign for engaging young voters through social media. They detailed how the campaign's use of memes, especially around the "brat" theme, was energizing Democrats and bringing a level of excitement to the race. In "How Kamala Harris became part of Charli XCX's 'Brat' summer," NBC News described how Harris's campaign was "plugged in" to popular culture in a way that previous Democratic candidates hadn't been, noting the refreshing change for voters. They cited the enthusiasm this generated among young people and social media creators. A WIRED article titled "Kamala Harris' Brat Summer Is Almost Over. What's Next?" featured a discussion on how Harris's campaign was harnessing social media in innovative ways, with writer Hunter Harris (I assume no relation) commenting on the campaign's social media strategy being more nimble than Biden's, suggesting this could sustain her momentum.

Do you notice how all these media outlets seemed to write the same articles with the same messages? Fascinating, isn't it?

The embarrassing fawning over the infantile and insipid "Brat Summer" narrative served as a clear and unambiguous signal that the rest of the campaign journalists planned to abandon even a pretext of objectivity or critical analysis of the new Democrat ticket. They were on board and planned to celebrate anything the Harris campaign told them to celebrate. They had an election to win and they were on board to do whatever they would have to do to drag Harris across the finish line - even if it meant Jake Tapper would pledge to "aspire to be brat."

Chapter Eight - Charlottesville, Bloodbath and Dictator on Day One

"He said there were, quote, 'some very fine people on both sides.' Very fine people on both sides? With those words, the president of the United States assigned a moral equivalence between those spreading hate and those with the courage to stand against it. And in that moment I knew the threat to this nation was unlike any I had ever seen in my lifetime." - Joe Biden campaign announcement video, April 2019

Joe Biden claims that he ran for president in 2020 because of Donald Trump's statements after the Charlottesville, VA "Unite the Right" rally that ended in the vehicular homicide of a counter-protester named Hannah Graham. Biden claimed, at the time, that for the first time in American history, neo-Nazis and white supremacist Klansmen were referred to as "very fine people." Given his own fondness for former KKK kingpin-turned elder statesman of the Democrat Party Robert Byrd, it's hard to believe that it was the "first time in American history" a politician had said such a thing.

In fact, Democrat President Woodrow Wilson famously screened the Klan-sympathetic film "Birth of a Nation" at the White House, and the KKK played a key role in the Democratic Party nominating convention in 1924, known as the "Klanbake." Indeed, given the Democrats' long-time affinity for slavery, the Confederacy, and the KKK, it seems quite impossible that calling Klansmen "very fine people" would've been anything historic… that is if Trump had ever said such a thing. Which he did not.

Trump made the comments during a press conference on August 15, 2017, discussing the violence at the Charlottesville "Unite the Right" rally. He stated there were "very fine people on both sides," referring to those protesting the removal of the Robert E. Lee statue and counter-protesters. However, he explicitly condemned neo-Nazis and white supremacists in the same statement, saying they should be "condemned totally."

"But you also had people that were very fine people, on both sides. You had people in that group that were there to protest the taking down of, to them, a very, very important statue, and the renaming of a park from Robert E. Lee to another

name. ***I'm not talking about the neo-Nazis and the white nationalists, because they should be condemned totally.*** But you had many people in that group other than neo-Nazis and white nationalists, okay? And the press has treated them absolutely unfairly."

Not that the legacy media ever took the time to tell the truth about this incident. The most "trusted news outlets" from CNN to the *New York Times* to *The Washington Post* all lied about what Trump said, and what he didn't say.

The *New York Times*: An article headline stated, "Trump Gives White Supremacists an Unequivocal Boost," implied that Trump directly endorsed white supremacists.

CNN: Multiple CNN articles and broadcasts referred to Trump's comments as suggesting that there were "fine people" among the neo-Nazis and white supremacists. For instance, one headline was, "Trump says both sides to blame amid Charlottesville backlash," which could mislead readers into thinking Trump equated the two groups without clarifying that he was speaking about different factions involved in the rally, not the neo-Nazis specifically.

MSNBC: Rachel Maddow on MSNBC commented that Trump had "refused to condemn" the white supremacists in Charlottesville, when he clearly had done exactly that.

The Washington Post: An opinion piece titled "Trump's 'very fine people' comments on Charlottesville, explained" suggested Trump was talking about neo-Nazis when he said "very fine people," even though Trump explicitly stated he was *not* talking about neo-Nazis and white nationalists.

In 2024, while running for re-election, Biden continued to repeat the same Charlottesville "very fine people" lie with his vivid "veins bulging" embellishments to justify his run for re-election and to further demonize his opponent. For the most part, the media allowed the lies to continue without so much as a footnote.

"Would you place your faith in someone who instituted a so-called Muslim ban, or sat down with Holocaust deniers, or said that there were "very fine people on both sides" of a white supremacist rally?" Barack Obama, November 3, 2024, Wisconsin Campaign Rally

Remarkably though, there was one outlier to the legacy media monopoly on the "very fine people" propaganda. Snopes, is a "fact-checking" website first established to debunk Internet myths and legends, but has now largely become a left-leaning political "fact-check" clearing house to equivocate liberal attacks and to "debunk" conservative-based assertions. On June 20, 2024, Snopes published an article titled "No, Trump Did Not Call Neo-Nazis and White Supremacists 'Very Fine

People'" where they rated the claim that Trump called neo-Nazis and white supremacists "very fine people" as "False." This was a significant shift from earlier interpretations or implications in media coverage that Trump had equated or praised neo-Nazis.

The change by Snopes was met with both support and criticism. Some viewed it as Snopes correcting a long-standing misrepresentation, while others argued that Snopes was too lenient or missed the broader implications of Trump's rhetoric. For the most part, the legacy media brands ignored the correction and continued to allow the lies made by both politicians and media figures. The "very fine people" legend, it appears, will forever be included in the left's arsenal of misinformation against Trump and his supporters.

"Now, if I don't get elected, it's going to be a bloodbath for the country." - Donald Trump March 16, 2024, Ohio

The statement, at a political rally, was part of a broader discussion on the U.S. auto manufacturing industry and trade policies with China. The Trump campaign emphasized that the term "bloodbath" was meant in an economic context, specifically regarding the impact on the auto industry if Trump were not elected.

He specifically said:

"We're going to put a 100% tariff on every single car that comes across the line, and you're not going to be able to sell those cars if I get elected. Now if I don't get elected, it's going to be a bloodbath for the whole — that's going to be the least of it. It's going to be a bloodbath for the country. That'll be the least of it. But they're not going to sell those cars, they're building massive factories."

The fake media outrage was nearly immediate.

NBC News: An article headline stated, "Trump says there will be a 'bloodbath' if he loses the election," which suggested a threat of violence without providing immediate context that Trump was discussing the auto industry. The article later included the context, but the headline alone was a misleading abomination.

The *New York Times*: The headline "Trump Defends His Warning of a 'Blood Bath for the Country'" similarly focused on the term "blood bath" without directly linking it to the auto industry in the headline, which could imply a broader threat.

ABC News: Their reporting included headlines like "Trump says there will be 'bloodbath' if he loses 2024 election, ramps up anti-migrant rhetoric," which again emphasized the term "bloodbath" without immediate context in the headline, leading to interpretations of violence rather than economic disaster.

Politico: An article headlined "Trump says country faces 'bloodbath' if Biden wins in November" again, focusing on the term "bloodbath" in a way that suggested political unrest or violence rather than strictly economic consequences. The body of the article provided more context, but the headline was all *Politico* needed to get the message across.

Various users on X (formerly Twitter) expressed frustration over what they perceived as media manipulation. For instance, one post criticized how media outlets like MSNBC and CNN described staff changes at the RNC as a "bloodbath" but interpreted Trump's use of the word differently, exposing the double standard in media portrayal.

"Donald Trump, the candidate, has said, in this election, there will be a bloodbath if the outcome of this election is not to his liking." - Kamala Harris during the ABC News Presidential Debate

It was a lie, They all knew it was a lie. There were plenty of emboldened conservative analysts, columnists, and journalists who kept pointing out the lie, yet they continued to repeat it. Right up until election day.

"Dictator on Day One"

I continue to believe that one of the biggest reasons the Washington DC media have such trouble covering Donald Trump is because they still don't understand that he is incredibly funny.

Trump's ability to "go off prompter" at his rallies and riff on whatever topic he cared to riff about was unparalleled in modern American politics. Like a stream-of-consciousness stand-up comedian, Trump can zig and zag and weave a hilarious monologue on serious political issues and not only communicate big ideas to his audience but leave them in stitches as well. Perhaps the talent was honed in his days as a network television superstar hosting *The Apprentice* and *The Celebrity Apprentice* for NBC. Or, perhaps, he picked up the gift from so many marathon negotiation settings in Manhattan board rooms - where the powerful charm and disarm each other with their fascinating anecdotes. Maybe it goes back to his college days at Wharton School of Business.

Wherever Trump learned the skill, he's got it. And he is one funny guy. You just can't help but laugh at his delivery and his material… unless you are one of the die-hard, Trump Derangement Syndrome victims who obsessively loathe his every utterance. Trump's humor and his instinct to always go for the quick laugh while communicating ideas in a rally or interview setting was on full display when he sat for an exchange with Fox News host Sean Hannity.

During a town hall event in Iowa on December 5, 2023, Hannity asked Trump if he would promise not to abuse power as retribution against anybody if re-elected, to which Trump responded with his "day one" dictator remark.

HANNITY: "I want to go back to this one issue though because the media has been focused on this and attacking you. Under no circumstances you're promising America tonight you would never abuse power as retribution against anybody?"

TRUMP: "Except for Day 1."

HANNITY: "Except for?"

TRUMP: (pointing to Hannity) "Look, he's going crazy. Except for Day 1."

HANNITY: "Meaning?"

TRUMP: "I want to close the border and I want to drill, drill, drill."

HANNITY: "That's not retribution."

TRUMP (referring to Hannity): "We love this guy. He says, 'You are not going to be a dictator, are you?' I said, 'No, no, no, other than Day 1.' We are closing the border and we are drilling, drilling, drilling. After that I am not a dictator, OK?"

Now, clearly, Trump was saying that on his first day in office, and only his first day in office, he would engage in executive actions, within the traditional and constitutional power of the presidency, to achieve important goals. It was clear to anyone listening at the time that his seeming affirmation of Hannity's "Dictator" characterization was a hyperbolic and humorous affectation to deliver an emphatic message. Only a disingenuous, deceitful hack would report that Trump intended to be a dictator should he be elected president, right?

The Atlantic: Trump Says He'll Be a Dictator on 'Day One'

The Guardian: Trump says he will be a dictator only on 'day one' if elected president

AP: Trump's vow to only be a dictator on 'day one' follows growing worry over his authoritarian rhetoric

NPR: During the campaign, Trump promised to be a dictator — but only for a day.

The Washington Post: Trump says he wouldn't be a dictator 'except for Day One'.

ABC News: "Trump raised new alarms last year when he referred to himself as a 'dictator' but only on 'Day 1' during a town hall in Iowa."

CBS News: "Former President Donald Trump said Tuesday in Fox News Town Hall that he would not be a dictator 'except for Day One' if he is elected to the presidency next year."

NBC News: "Former President Donald Trump said at a Fox News town hall Tuesday that he would not be a dictator 'except for Day One' if he is elected president next year."

The charge was repeated over and over and over again by Democrats on the stump and by journalists doing their bidding. It was repeated so many times it was just taken for granted that it was the fact. Though it clearly was not.

The "Dictator on Day One" lie was often regurgitated in the same sentence as the other "Very Fine People" and "Bloodbath" lies. The media wove these prevarications into their television scripts and campaign trail articles with ease and aplomb. The lies became conventional wisdom-fact. It was so insidious that the very few pro-Trump conservative television analysts who attempted to fact-check the assertions on television panels would be shouted down and ridiculed. The lies were repeated so often the truth no longer mattered.

The media knew better and they didn't care or they literally thought these lies were true. Either way, they were engaged in the most despicable form of misinformation to their audience at the height of a presidential campaign. Their priorities were not information and fact, their priority was to harm Trump, by any means necessary. And so, the "Very Fine

People/Bloodbath/Dictator on Day One" lies stuck and will probably find their way into history books in the coming years.

Even though none of it was ever true in the first place.

Chapter Nine - 60 Minutes Runs Out of Time

"Sir, let me tell you something: This is 60 Minutes, and we can't put on things that we can't verify." -
Leslie Stahl to Donald Trump, October 2020

The pinnacle (or nadir) of the corporate media propagandists' attempts to promote Kamala Harris and defeat Donald Trump in the 2024 presidential campaign came in the form of the most traditional, presidential media rites of passage of the past several decades: The *60 Minutes* interview.

In every presidential cycle, going back to the 1970s, every presidential candidate was expected to make the pilgrimage to the set of *60 Minutes*, the grand-daddy of "serious" and "important" news shows and a fixture on CBS (the 'Tiffany Network') on Sunday Nights. For journalists, *60 Minutes* is not the gold standard, it's the platinum standard (or whatever metal is more precious these days). And for politicians, *60 Minutes* is either the opportunity to be accepted and welcomed into the elite of political circles by the gatekeepers in New York and Washington, or it's a deathtrap waiting to end the hopes and dreams of pretenders trying to fly too close to the sun only to be brought down to earth by the likes of Mike Wallace or Ed Bradley or Leslie Stahl. *60 Minutes* is the biggest of big leagues and it's not even debatable: If you want to be President, you must submit yourself to *60 Minutes* for their crucible of an interview.

In 2024, Donald Trump rejected this premise. He flipped the conventional acceptance of *60 Minutes*' dominance on its head. He snubbed the show and ridiculed their attempts to sway the election. And, naturally, he won. He ended the *60 Minutes* monopoly on journalistic legitimacy - a monopoly they never really deserved in the first place. Trump exposed their partisanship and their hypocrisy. But, to be fair, *60 Minutes* did most of the hard work all by themselves.

Harris had avoided media interviews for weeks after assuming the throne of the Democratic Party nomination. For the first several weeks, her avoidance strategy was rationalized because, after all, she had been thrust into this role to save the party when Biden suddenly withdrew. She had more important things to do than an interview, she had to piece together a campaign from scratch with little or no time at all.

That story seemed to stick until Harris began sitting with social media influencers like Rayvone Grant, Amanda Seales, and Jemele Hill at the Democratic convention rather than a traditional "news" interview. Then it was clear she had plenty of time to sit for an interview, she just didn't want to. After a less-than-spectacular sit-down (with Tim Walz by her side) with CNN's Dana Bash, and then a halting one-on-one exchange with MSNBC's Stephanie Ruehl, Harris was ready to sit with Bill Whitaker of the venerable news magazine for a 40 minute interview.

Well, sort of. The 40 minute interview was eventually edited down to a 20 minute presentation for the CBS News viewers, but, nevertheless, Harris was submitting herself to the torture chamber that is a serious and hard-hitting *60 Minutes* interview so, she should be commended, right?

Yeah, right.

The interview took place on Thursday, October 3rd and was scheduled to broadcast in a prime-time special on Monday, October 7th. The first indications of how the famously-awkward California Democrat performed in the interview came Sunday morning when CBS News released a short clip on their Sunday show, *Face the Nation*, and on social media. The exchange focused on Harris' national security position, specifically as it related to Israel, Prime Minister Benjamin

Netanyahu and the ongoing conflict between Israel and the terror group, Hamas.

The teaser clip showed Harris giving a lengthy, somewhat convoluted response to Whitaker's challenge that Netanyahu didn't seem to be responding to the Biden/Harris's admonition to reduce civilian casualties in the Gaza territories in their efforts to root out Hamas terrorists - who famously hid within civilian enclaves to protect themselves or to create PR narratives should civilian casualties emerge after an attempt to root the terrorists out.

Here is the transcript of the 2:38 teaser clip that ran on Face the Nation:

WHITAKER: We supply Israel with billions of dollars in military aid, and yet, Prime Minister Netanyahu seems to be charting his own course. The Biden-Harris administration has pressed him to agree to a ceasefire. He's resisted. You urged him not to go into Lebanon. He went in anyway. He has promised to make Iran pay for the missile attack, and that has the potential of expanding the war. Does the U.S. have no sway over Prime Minister Netanyahu?

HARRIS: The aid that we have given Israel allowed Israel to defend itself against 200 ballistic missiles that were just meant to attack the Israelis and the people of Israel, and when we think about the threat that Hamas, Hezbollah, presents, um, Iran, um, I think that it is without any question our imperative to do what we can to allow Israel to defend itself against those kinds of attacks. Now, the work that we do diplomatically with the leadership of Israel is an ongoing pursuit around making clear our principles which include the need for humanitarian aid, the need for this war to end, the need for a deal to be done, which would release the hostages, and, and, and create a ceasefire, and we're not going to stop in terms of putting that pressure on Israel and, and in the region, including Arab leaders.

WHITAKER: But it seems that Prime Minister Netanyahu is not listening.

HARRIS: Well, Bill, the work that we have done has resulted in a number of movements in that region by Israel that were very much prompted by or a result of many things including our advocacy for what needs to happen in the region.

WHITAKER: Do we have a, a, a real close ally in Prime Minister Netanyahu?

HARRIS: I think, with all due respect, the better question is, do we have an important alliance between the American people and the Israeli people, and the answer to that question is yes.

The clip was classic Kamala. Word salad nonsense that was meant to sound intelligent but when actually analyzed was nothing more than platitudes and buzzwords that meant literally nothing and communicated even less. To call this answer "word salad" really isn't fair to salad. Salad at least has some nutritional value. If anything, it acts as roughage to help clear out what might be slow-going in your digestive system. This answer didn't even provide that side benefit. In fact, one felt a little constipated after viewing this dangerously inept exchange.

All day Sunday and through Monday, the clip went viral and Harris was mocked on social media and on conservative media platforms. Talk radio and conservative outlets particularly honed in on this exchange at the tail end of the teaser clip:

WHITAKER: But it seems that Prime Minister Netanyahu is not listening.

HARRIS: Well, Bill, the work that we have done has resulted in a number of movements in that region by Israel that were very much prompted by or a result of many things including our advocacy for what needs to happen in the region.

She looked out of her depth and, in the context of the subject at hand, she looked dangerous. Dangerous to our allies and dangerous to our own country. That Monday evening, during the actual "*60 Minutes*" broadcast, something miraculous (for Harris) happened. Her answer to the Israel/Netanyahu question was... different.

Harris's answer to the same question was edited to be shorter and more succinct. It was more coherent and made a little more sense. It also conveyed a slightly more stable characterization of her ever-evolving and nascent foreign policy. It was good enough to assuage voters who may have been worried about her lack of experience on the world stage.

Here is the transcript of the same exchange as it appeared in the final produced airing of the interview broadcast on *60 Minutes* Monday evening: (Modified edit in **bold**)

WHITAKER: We supply Israel with billions of dollars in military aid, and yet Prime Minister Netanyahu seems to be charting his own course. The Biden-Harris administration has pressed him to agree to a ceasefire. He's resisted. You urged him not to go into Lebanon. He went in anyway. Does the U.S. have no sway over Prime Minister Netanyahu?

HARRIS: The work that we do diplomatically with the leadership of Israel is an ongoing pursuit around making clear our principles.

WHITAKER: But it seems that Prime Minister Netanyahu is not listening.

HARRIS: We are not gonna stop pursuing what is necessary for the United States to be clear about where we stand on the need for this war to end.

WHITAKER: Do we have a, a, a real close ally in Prime Minister Netanyahu?

HARRIS: I think, with all due respect, the better question is, do we have an important alliance between the American people and the Israeli people, and the answer to that question is yes.

It doesn't take a trained eye to see what the team of editors at *60 Minutes* did. They chopped up her lengthy and disjointed answer and moved a sentence down from almost a minute earlier in the exchange, completely replacing the already-viral and endlessly mocked "word salad" answer, making it appear as though Harris was much more coherent and succinct than she actually was.

The reaction was swift and thorough. Now that the X platform was free of Twitter censorship and talk radio, podcasters and streaming shows were gaining larger and larger audiences, *60 Minutes* was no longer safe from their sacrosanct safety within the chummy world of professional, Democrat-approved journalism.

They got lambasted, lampooned and ridiculed.

Media analysts at The Federalist were particularly pointed in their attack. Election Correspondent Breccan F. Thies wrote:

Last week, CBS put on one of the most blatant attempts to deceive the American people by releasing one, and then a second totally different, answer to the same question. In the first version, Harris shared what has been widely mocked as a lengthy "word salad" answer to "60 Minutes" interviewer Bill Whitaker's question about Israel Prime Minister Benjamin Netanyahu's strained relationship with the White House.

The "word salad," however, did not make it into the edit that aired in the full interview, as it was replaced by a shorter, more succinct answer that did not appear in the first clip. The switcheroo, which appeared to be nothing less than corporate media election interference, earned scorn and even a Federal Communications Commission (FCC) complaint accusing CBS of "significant and intentional news distortion."

"This isn't just about one interview or one network," Daniel Suhr, president of the Center for American Rights, which filed *the complaint, said in a statement. "This is about the public's trust in the media on critical issues of national security and international relations during one of the most consequential elections of our time."*

"When broadcasters manipulate interviews and distort reality, it undermines democracy itself. The FCC must act swiftly to restore public confidence in our news media," Suhr added.

On October 10th, Trump called it a "giant Fake News Scam by CBS & *60 Minutes*," stating that Harris's "REAL ANSWER WAS CRAZY, OR DUMB," and they replaced it to make her look better. He demanded that CBS lose its license, describing the action as "Election Interference."

On October 14th, Trump suggested that Kamala Harris should pass a test on Cognitive Stamina and Agility, criticizing the editing by saying CBS and *60 Minutes* "illegally and unscrupulously replaced" her answer to protect her.

On October 21st, Trump demanded that CBS release the transcript of the interview, accusing CBS of changing Harris's answer to make her "look intelligent, rather than 'dumb as a rock.'" He referred to this as potentially, "the Biggest Scandal in Broadcast History!"

In response to Trump and others calling for the full 40-minute interview transcript to be released so it could be compared to the edited and pared-down 20-minute broadcast piece, *60 Minutes* issued the following statement:

"Former President Donald Trump is accusing 60 Minutes of deceitful editing of our Oct. 7, 2024 segment featuring Vice President Kamala Harris. That is false. 60 Minutes gave an excerpt of our interview to Face the Nation that used a longer section of her answer than that on 60 Minutes. Same question. Same answer. But a different portion of the response. When we edit any interview, whether a politician, an athlete, or movie star, we strive to be clear, accurate and on point. The portion of her answer on 60 Minutes was more succinct, which allows time for other subjects in a wide ranging 21-minute-long segment. Remember, Mr. Trump pulled out of his interview with 60 Minutes and the vice president participated. Our long-standing invitation to former President Trump remains open. If he would like to discuss the issues facing the nation and the Harris interview, we would be happy to have him on 60 Minutes."

The disingenuous attempt to turn the issue back on Trump and make it appear he was in some way intimidated or scared to appear on the program was transparent and laughable. *60 Minutes* was not communicating to a skeptical public about their standards and practices, they were engaged in a political back-and-forth with a presidential candidate in a game of chicken. They were behaving exactly like you would expect an entity populated by political operatives with a campaign agenda to behave. Because that's precisely what they are.

Calls to release the full transcript began to resonate.

Will Scharf, an attorney for President Donald J. Trump, penned a scathing opinion piece in The Federalist:

CBS News was once one of the defining news outlets in the world. Whether it was Edward R. Murrow reporting live from London during the Blitz in World War II or Walter Cronkite's coverage of the assassination of President John F. Kennedy, generations of Americans turned to CBS for fair, accurate reporting on the most important issues of the day.

No longer.

CBS News now stands accused of deliberately distorting its news coverage for nakedly political purposes, to prop up Kamala Harris' flailing presidential campaign by attempting to hide her inability to answer even simple questions about her policy positions and how she would act if elected president.

Scharf then reminded readers of *60 Minutes* and CBS News past attempts to interfere with presidential elections:

Unfortunately, CBS is no stranger to election-rigging news controversies. On Sept. 8, 2004, at the height of that contentious presidential election, "60 Minutes" anchor Dan Rather breathlessly covered the damning "Killian memos," which purported to prove that President George W. Bush had shirked his responsibilities to the Texas Air National Guard decades earlier. The only problem was that the Killian memos were quickly proven by internet sleuths to be clumsy modern-day forgeries. Rather was quickly put out to pasture and staffers were fired, but clearly CBS did not learn its lesson — its willingness to distort the truth for nakedly political purposes remains apparently unaltered two decades later.

Former CBS News investigative journalist Catherine Herridge joined the calls for the full transcript to be released and pointed to past precedent as more than ample rationale for CBS News to deflect the charges of election interference by simply being transparent. CBS had previously released the full transcript of her interview with Donald Trump in 2020, emphasizing that it was "about transparency and standing behind the integrity of the final edit." She argued for the same standard to be applied to Harris's interview, stating that releasing the unedited transcript would help clarify any discrepancies and uphold journalistic integrity.

Herridge also noted in various posts and articles that this was not an isolated incident, as CBS had released full transcripts for interviews with other figures like former Attorney General Bill Barr and Federal Reserve Chair Jerome Powell. She criticized CBS for not following through with the same level of transparency for Harris's interview, suggesting that it was inconsistent with their established practices.

The calls for the full release of the Harris transcript fell on deaf ears at CBS News. As of the publication of this book (January 2025) the transcript was still hidden from the public's view. *60 Minutes* maintained their position through the entire controversy that they had done nothing wrong, but their smarmy insistence that Trump could have his say if only he agreed to sit for an interview with the news magazine was especially disingenuous and manipulative.

To understand just how loathsome CBS News was being with their obsequious "Remember, Mr. Trump pulled out of his interview ... we would be happy to have him on *60 Minutes*," we must recall the last time Trump agreed to play the *60 Minutes* game during the 2020 presidential election. The interview was filmed on October 20, 2020, and was set to air on October 25, 2020. CBS News correspondent Lesley Stahl had her crew set up in The Roosevelt Room of the White House for the 38 minute interview.

The Trump campaign (and the White House archivists) recorded the entire exchange and the Trump campaign released the entire recording they had made so it could be compared with the edited version *60 Minutes* finally presented. The edited segment that aired on CBS focused on several contentious exchanges, particularly around Trump's handling of the coronavirus and his public criticisms of Dr. Anthony Fauci, suggesting Fauci had been wrong about many things regarding the lockdown, (an undeniable fact with 2024 hindsight, but in 2020, Fauci was sacrosanct) and the media's refusal to report on the scandals whirling around Biden and his son, Hunter. Before the edited version aired on CBS, Trump released the unedited footage on his social media, accusing Stahl of bias, harshness, and constant interruptions. This move was unprecedented, as the White House had agreed to use the footage only for archival purposes.

CBS criticized Trump's decision to leak the footage, stating it violated their agreement. Nonetheless, they affirmed their commitment to airing the interview with (according to them) full, fair, and contextual reporting. The most significant portion of the conversation revolved around the Hunter Biden scandals. Trump brought up the topic of Hunter Biden's emails, which had become a focal point of controversy due to the New York Post's reporting on the contents of a laptop belonging to Hunter Biden. At the time of the airing, the media had bought the lie that the story and the laptop itself were products of Russian disinformation. The notion was attested to by fifty-one "intelligence community professionals."

"I think that we have more than enough for an interview," Trump said at one point. "I think that when we talk about Hunter, you can't get away from the fact that he was getting money from Russia, from China, from Ukraine."

"But that's not what this is about," Stahl responded. She seemed to dismiss the topic or at least indicated a lack of interest in pursuing it deeply, which led to Trump's frustration.

"Why aren't you covering the biggest political scandal in the history of our country?" Trump asked, incredulously.

"Well, because it can't be verified," she insisted.

"Oh, come on! It has been totally verified," Trump correctly asserted. "And you know it has been. And you refuse to cover it. And you know who the laptop belongs to. You know who it is."

"This is the most important issue in the country right now?" Stahl asks about two-thirds of the way into the interview.

"It's a very important issue to find out whether a man's corrupt who's running for president, who's accepted money from China, and Ukraine, and from Russia," Trump responds. "Take a look at what's going on, Leslie, and you say that shouldn't be discussed?...I think it's one of the biggest scandals I've ever seen, and you don't cover it."

"Well because it can't be verified," Stahl says. "I'm telling you—"

"Of course it can be verified," Trump interjects. "Excuse me, Leslie, they found a laptop—"

"It can't be verified," Stahl repeats.

Earlier in the interview, Stahl also said there was "no evidence" that the FBI spied on the 2016 Trump campaign.

"The biggest scandal was when they spied on my campaign. They spied on my campaign," Trump said.

"There's no evidence of that," Stahl responded.

"Of course there is, it's all over the place. Leslie, they spied on my campaign and they got caught," Trump went on.

"Sir, let me tell you something. This is *60 Minutes*, and we can't put on things that we can't verify," Stahl said.

Eventually, Trump walked out of the interview and his full version was juxtaposed against *60 Minutes*' edited version. So, given *60 Minutes*' past behavior with Trump, and now their 2024 effort to edit their interview with Kamala Harris to make her answers look more coherent and intelligent, it's pretty easy to see why Trump would refuse to go on their show and why he would scream bloody murder over this latest episode. For *60 Minutes* to pretend that they were merely following standard editing practices and to innocently invite Trump on their show to have his say, after their outrageous Stahl interview of 2020, is the absolute epitome of media arrogance.

To be clear: CBS News' efforts to whitewash Kamala Harris' word salad to clean-up her answer and make her appear more presidential than the babbling fool she appeared to be was nothing more than outright election interference. It was election interference wrapped in the protective cloak of "journalism" and "freedom of the press." And Trump's criticisms were characterized as causing a "chilling effect" on press freedom.   Absolute Insanity.

Chapter Ten - A Tale of Two Veeps

Nothing could better illustrate the media lies of the 2024 presidential campaign than a full analysis of how, as a monolith, they covered the two respective running mates Ohio Senator J.D. Vance and Minnesota Governor Tim Walz. Donald Trump picked Vance as his vice-presidential running mate on July 15, 2024.

James David Vance was born on August 2, 1984, in Middletown, Ohio. His birthdate makes him the first member of the "Millennial" generation to enter national politics on a presidential ticket. This, obviously, was ignored by the media where it would've been ballyhooed for days should the first millennial identified as a Democrat. Republicans, you see, aren't allowed to be *young*, let alone generational figures.

Vance was raised in impoverished, rural Appalachia. He chronicled his mother's struggles with addiction and his childhood odyssey from being raised by his grandmother to his formation in the United States Marine Corps in the best-selling book, "Hillbilly Elegy: A Memoir of a Family and Culture in Crisis" in 2016. Director Ron Howard adapted it into an award-winning film starring Glenn Close and Amy Adams. The book (along with Vance) was hailed for its insights into the struggles of America's white working class. Hillbilly Elegy was often referenced as a "Rosetta Stone" of sorts by elite Manhattan journalists who didn't fully understand the resentment of the Midwest states against Obama and the Democrats, which led to Trump's shocking victory in 2016. Because of his insights, Vance was a frequent guest on left-leaning cable news programs to "explain" Trump voters to the viewers and to the hosts.

After the Marine Corps, Vance received a Bachelor's degree in Political Science and Philosophy from Ohio State University and then, a Juris Doctor from Yale Law School. After law school, Vance worked in Silicon Valley, including stints at Peter Thiel's Mithril Capital Management. Through the Trump presidency (a presidency he was initially skeptical of) Vance transitioned into conservative commentary and political activism, appearing frequently on Fox News to discuss social issues - particularly those affecting rural and working-class America.

In 2021, he entered politics by running for and winning a U.S. Senate seat from Ohio as a Republican, defeating the incumbent Democrat Sherrod Brown. As a senator, he has focused on issues like addiction recovery, veterans' affairs, and economic development in rural areas.

Vance is married to Usha Chilukuri, a Yale Law School classmate, and they have three children together.

On paper, he was a unique, fresh, and ground-breaking choice for Trump to make. Known for his critique of both political parties, Vance had positioned himself as a voice for conservative populism, emphasizing cultural and economic revitalization in America's heartland. J.D. Vance's journey from a memoirist capturing the American zeitgeist to a central figure in Republican politics underscored his significant influence on contemporary American political allegiances and the shifting politics of the political parties.

The media reaction was almost unanimously negative.

The framing of their analysis was almost entirely focused on Trump picking Vance to "shore up his MAGA base" which made virtually no sense since Trump's "MAGA base was completely committed to walking over hot coals to vote for the President, not Vance. Alternatively, the focus was on Vance's "transformation" from Trump skeptic in 2016 to "extreme

MAGA acolyte" in his "cynical" political ambition to be a senator and, eventually, president.

NBC News: "Trump picks Sen. JD Vance as his vice presidential running mate in 2024 election"

NBC News highlighted Vance's transformation from a Trump critic to a loyalist, obsessing over his appeal to Trump's base. The article emphasized Vance's youth, his military service, and his populist views aligning with Trump's "America First" slogan. It also discussed how Vance could help in battleground states surrounding Ohio.

BBC News: "Who is Trump's vice-president, JD Vance?"

The BBC focused on Vance's personal story from "Hillbilly Elegy," his shift from a "never-Trumper" to a MAGA champion, and his "controversial views" on immigration and foreign policy. They noted his potential as the "early frontrunner" for the 2028 presidential nomination.

ABC News: "Trump picks JD Vance as 2024 running mate"

ABC News described Vance as a "young, ideological ally" whose selection was meant to energize Trump's base. They pointed out the strategic nature of choosing Vance, who had emerged as a staunch Trump supporter in the Senate. The article also included reactions from other political figures like Jen O'Malley Dillon from the Biden campaign, who criticized the pick as an endorsement of Trump's "extreme MAGA agenda."

Reuters: "JD Vance once compared Trump to Hitler. Now, he is Trump's vice president-elect"

Reuters emphasized the irony of Vance's past criticisms of Trump, including comparing him to Hitler, juxtaposed with his current role. They discussed Vance's evolution in political stance, his work on issues like the East Palestine train derailment, and his fundraising efforts for Trump. The article also highlighted the implications for the Republican Party's future.

The *New York Times*: "How J.D. Vance Won Over Donald Trump"

The NYT provided a detailed account of how Vance managed to transition from Trump's critic to his running mate. It included anecdotes like Vance's initial meeting with Trump at Mar-a-Lago and the support from key Trump allies like Tucker Carlson and Elon Musk.

Vance's nomination *should* have been met with intelligent and insightful analysis of his transformational status as the first millennial on a national ticket his insights from rural Appalachia and the changing identities of Republican voters breaking out of the stereotypical "country club" identity of the past several decades. Instead, the media wrote him off as being "too Trumpy" and that was pretty much it. That is until they had a new narrative to play with.

When Minnesota Gov. Tim Walz called Vance "weird." Then, everything changed.

On July 23rd, Minnesota Governor and then-Democratic vice-presidential hopeful Tim Walz appeared on MSNBC's "*Morning Joe*." During this interview, Walz discussed the Democratic strategy for the 2024 election and the importance of focusing on shared values like strong public schools, healthcare, and labor unions.

The interview was part of the buildup to the Democratic National Convention and Walz's potential as a running mate for Kamala Harris, especially following Biden's withdrawal from the race.

Walz pivoted to Vance, the newly-named Trump running mate. He described Vance as someone who "knows nothing about small-town America," an astonishingly laughable comment considering Vance *literally* was best known for writing *Hillbilly Elegy* fully focused on small-town America.

Believe it or not, the MSNBC hosts failed to point this out to the Governor. Walz used this critique to contrast himself with Vance, emphasizing his own background in education and service in the military, which he argued gave him a better understanding of middle America's values and needs.

Walz was clearly auditioning to be Harris' running mate.

Then, he pretty much locked up the job by calling Vance "weird."

"These guys are just weird. They're running for He-Man women haters club or something. That's what they go at. That's not what people are interested in."

Whether it was off-the-cuff, premeditated, or even scripted by the Harris campaign, it landed.

Walz's use of "weird" was part of a broader narrative by Democrats to paint Vance as an unusual figure in politics. He particularly focused on Vance's past comments on women (childless cat ladies making policies for the rest of us), his views on abortion (he thought babies shouldn't be killed in utero), and his business success which, according to Walz, illustrated a disconnect from rural and small-town American life. Walz's comments were extremely strategic, aiming to define Vance in the public eye as someone who doesn't represent or understand the average American, especially in contrast to Walz's own narrative of being a "public school teacher" and "Midwesterner."

The "weird" interview helped set the tone for Democratic rhetoric against Vance, with "weird" becoming a recurring theme in their campaign messaging. The interview was pivotal in amplifying the narrative, contributing to the political discourse around the vice-presidential candidates in the lead-up to the election. The talking point was defined and the media ran with it.

For the next several weeks, any cable or broadcast news discussion about Vance included the word "weird" multiple times. It was as if a memo had been delivered to every Manhattan producer with influence over new content in America. The script was set: If you talked about Vance, call him "weird." And boy did they.

Tom Elliott, founder of media aggregation site Grabien, documented the use of "weird" in connection with Vance's name from July 15 through July 29th across all cable and broadcast news shows. A total of 720 references to "weird" occurred with CNN and MSNBC leading the charge.

Serious journalistic endeavors like the *New York Times* naturally *celebrated* the use of name-calling in the presidential race. They ran an op-ed titled *"Trump Is 'Weird,' Vance Is 'Creepy.' Finally, the Democrats Start Name-Calling"* by Contributing Editor Jessica Bennet. Yes, the *New York Times*, a publication that spent years hand-wringing over Trump's hyperbolic jokes at rallies and name-calling of political rivals like "Crooked Hillary," "Sleepy Joe" and "Pocahontas" was now cheering Walz for calling a Marine Corps veteran, Yale graduate, and rags-to-riches self-made millionaire "weird."

Meanwhile, by any objective measure, it was Walz - Harris' eventual pick as running mate, who was decidedly weird.

On the strength of his cable news appearances, Harris named Walz as her running mate. A former school teacher from the Midwest, he was immediately painted by the propagandists on cable news as the "real deal" version of the pretend Midwesterner Vance tried to be. Walz wore flannel shirts, was a high-ranking, retired enlisted non-commissioned officer in the Army National Guard, and even coached his high school football team to a state championship. Take that, Vance, you weirdo.

Of course, almost immediately, these storylines were revealed to be hyperbolic fiction and the reality of Tim Walz's past was very strange, and virtually ignored by the watchdogs of the 4th estate.

DUI Arrest: Walz was arrested for drunk driving in 1995 in Nebraska when he was a teacher. He was caught speeding at 96 mph in a 55 mph zone and had a blood alcohol level above the legal limit. He pleaded guilty to a reduced charge of reckless driving.

Initially, his congressional campaign in 2006 provided misleading information, claiming he wasn't drunk and attributing his behavior to a hearing impairment. Later, Walz acknowledged the incident and said it was a life-changing event that led him to stop drinking.

Stolen Valor: Walz served in the U.S. Army National Guard and retired as a Command Sergeant Major, the highest rank an enlisted soldier can reach. It's the enlisted equivalent of being a general.

In reality, Walz retired as a Master Sergeant (a great achievement in and of itself), but he was often referred to, or referred to himself, as having retired as a Command Sergeant Major. This discrepancy led to accusations of "stolen valor." He was clearly guilty of exaggerating his military rank and service. Additionally, he was on video advocating for a so-called "assault weapons ban" by claiming Americans shouldn't be allowed to carry around the kind of guns he carried in combat, despite the fact that he never served in combat.

His overseas deployments had him serving in Europe *supporting* Operation Enduring Freedom but he never came close to serving in Afghanistan.

Handling of the 2020 George Floyd Protests: Walz was criticized for his response to the riots following George Floyd's death at the hands of a police officer in Minneapolis. He was slow to deploy the National Guard, leading to widespread destruction. His hands-off approach to the violent riots was an obvious attempt to appease his progressive base. He gladly allowed the city to burn before acting.

COVID-19 Response and Fraud: Walz implemented some of the strictest lockdown measures and mask mandates in the country during the COVID-19 pandemic. Meanwhile, there was a major fraud scandal involving the "Feeding Our Future" program, where over $250 million in federal aid was misappropriated on his watch.

He even implemented "snitch" hotlines encouraging Minnesotans to rat-out their neighbors if they engaged in any social interactions that violated Walz' draconian measures.

Cultural and Social Policies: Walz's progressive policies, like making Minnesota a refuge for transgender youth seeking medical care and enacting demonic laws on abortion made him the most radical cultural leftist in the nation.

With all of this, the media still tried to depict him as a regular guy with down-home, traditional midwestern values that real men should embrace. But the "weird" factor was only barely reflected in the above-referenced scandals and policy positions.

As a person… as a man… Walz was, there's no other word for it: Weird.

Jazz Hands and Gestures: Walz's hand movements while appearing at rallies and delivering remarks were wild and extremely animated. It wasn't long before conservative observers described them as "jazz hands." They were probably an attempt to convey enthusiasm but came off as distracting or excessive.

He looked just… weird.

Facial Expressions: Walz was often seen contorting his face during interviews with a "compression of lips," interpreted by some as withholding information or emotion, leading to speculation about his authenticity or comfort in the national spotlight. He was, you know, weird.

Overuse and incorrect use of sports analogies: Walz, who we we're constantly reminded was a former high school football coach, often relied heavily on sports analogies in his speeches and interviews. This was seen by some as an attempt to connect with Midwestern voters but was critiqued for being repetitive or simplistic in broader political contexts.

"Huddle up, America. Time for one last pep talk. It's the final quarter. But we've got the ball and the right team to win this," Walz posted on social media days before the election. Sen. Tommy Tuberville (R-AL), an *actual* college football coach-turned-senator, replied, "We call it the *4th* Quarter, 'Coach'."

Awkwardness in High-Pressure Situations: During debates and press conferences, Walz was observed to be visibly uncomfortable at times, with some commentators describing his behavior as "nervous" or "rusty." This was particularly highlighted after his performance in the vice-presidential debate, where his body language and fast-talking were seen as signs of discomfort or... Just downright weird.

Overcompensation: There was a perception that Walz was trying too hard to be likable or to fit into the national political arena, leading to actions or statements that seemed forced or out of character for him. His attempt at humor, including a J.D. Vance/couch-sex joke in his acceptance speech, was seen by some as inappropriate or misjudged for the setting and, well, you guessed it: WEIRD.

The point is, that the media repeated the political talking point that Vance was weird even though by any objective measure, Vance was the normalest of normies. Meanwhile, they ignored or downplayed all of Walz's bizarre behaviors and physical overcompensating that were obviously weird, and they pretended *he* was the normal one. More importantly, the champions of "speaking truth to power" ignored Walz' stolen valor claims, his DUI arrest and subsequent lies, and his unexplained multiple trips to communist China over the past several decades.

Vance was the quintessential, rags-to-riches American success story and they called him "weird" because the Harris campaign told them to. Walz was a mess and had a checkered if not corrupt past and they pretended he was normal because the Harris campaign told them to.

If you want to see how deceitful the American media was in the 2024 presidential campaign, just look at how they handled the two Vice Presidential candidates and you will see it all.

Chapter Eleven - Debate: Trump vs. ABC News

The 2024 presidential campaign was a turning point in how presidential debates would be conducted in the coming election cycles. Not just because of the biased, unfair moderation provided by ABC News, but for the mere fact that for the first time in decades, both campaigns agreed to bypass the now-defunct Commission on Presidential Debates. The Commission on Presidential Debates which had falsely presented itself as a bi-partisan (or even more deceptively a 'non-partisan') commission set up to determine the protocols for these debates had become a politicized, establishment dinosaur.

When the commission allowed their rules to be manipulated by the Biden campaign during the 2020 election over COVID protocols, (canceling one debate when Trump was diagnosed COVID-positive and adding a plexiglass wall between the candidates after Trump rejected their proposal for a "virtual" format for the final debate) Trump had sworn he'd bypass them in 2024, and he did. By ignoring the commission in 2024, Trump demonstrated that they were not necessary for the process to go forward. His campaign negotiated directly with the Biden campaign and the networks. They agreed to a total of three debates.

The first, in late June, turned out to be the end of the Biden campaign as his cognitive decline was so acute and demonstrable, the pressure from within his own party forced him off the ticket for good. The second, on ABC, and the third on Fox News. After Biden dropped out, Vice President Kamala Harris behaved as though she could assume the same conditions that Trump's team had negotiated with Biden. Trump demurred and suggested that negotiations would have to begin again. Harris and the media immediately claimed that Trump was "scared" to debate Harris by balking at the previously agreed upon debates.

Eventually, the two camps agreed to the ABC News debate and a CBS News Vice Presidential debate. Harris refused to participate in a debate that was to be moderated by Martha

MacCallum and Bret Baier on Fox News. The moderators for the ABC News debate were David Muir and Linsey Davis while the CBS News Veep debate would be hosted by Norah O'Donnell and Margaret Brennan. During the ABC News debate, on September 10, moderator David Muir interrupted the proceedings five times to "fact-check" Trump in real-time. The fact checks involved claims Trump made regarding crime, the economy, voter fraud, healthcare, and climate change.

In the spirit of brevity, we will only examine the first fact-check Muir employed against Trump, the exchange relating to crime statistics.

TRUMP: And all over the world crime is down. All over the world except here. Crime here is up and through the roof. Despite the fraudulent statements that they made. Crime in this country is through the roof. And we have a new form of crime. It's called migrant crime. And it's happening at levels that nobody thought possible.

MUIR: President Trump, as you know, the FBI says overall violent crime is coming down in this country, but Vice President the...

TRUMP: Excuse me, the FBI -- they were defrauding statements. They didn't include the worst cities. They didn't include the cities with the worst crime. It was a fraud. Just like the number of 818,000 jobs that they said they created turned out to be a fraud.

MUIR: President Trump, thank you. I'll let you respond, Vice President Harris.

The problem with Muir's "fact-check" was that the FBI crime statistics in question were from 2022, a year that had incomplete data, and Trump knew this as it had been widely reported in right-of-center media outlets, but not, apparently, on ABC News.

In May 2024, the Coalition for Law and Order published a study that pointed out that the FBI had to *estimate* crime statistics for major cities like New York, Los Angeles, Phoenix, and Pittsburgh due to their non-participation in the FBI's data survey. The study's authors, Mark Morgan, who was previously an assistant FBI director and is now the president of CLOS, along with Sean Kennedy, the executive director of CLOS, wrote in the Washington Examiner that these FBI statistics are potentially misleading or unreliable due to the gaps in reporting. They explained that because these cities didn't submit data via the NIBRS, the FBI resorted to making educated guesses to fill in the gaps, leading to uncertainties in the accuracy of the reported crime numbers. In fact, the FBI quietly revised their 2022 crime numbers in October, one month after the debate. You guessed it: They revised the numbers *up*.

Crime statistic expert Jon Lott noticed the adjustment and drew attention to it in an article on Real Clear Investigations:

When the FBI originally released the "final" crime data for 2022 in September 2023, it reported that the nation's violent crime rate fell by 2.1%. This quickly became and remains, a Democratic Party talking point to counter Donald Trump's claims of soaring crime.

But the FBI has quietly revised those numbers, releasing new data that shows violent crime increased in 2022 by 4.5%. The new data includes thousands more murders, rapes, robberies, and aggravated assaults...

...After the FBI released its new crime data in September, a USA Today headline read: "Violent crime dropped for third straight year in 2023, including murder and rape."

"I have checked the data on total violent crime from 2004 to 2022," Carl Moody, a professor at the College of William & Mary who specializes in studying crime, told RealClearInvestigations. "There were no revisions from 2004 to 2015, and from 2016 to 2020, there were small changes of less than one percentage point. The huge changes in 2021 and

2022, especially without an explanation, make it difficult to trust the FBI data."

In short, Trump was correct about crime. Muir was wrong. The fact-check was not a fact-check, it was interference in the debate and it was Muir, on behalf of ABC News, putting his foot on the scale and trying to assist Harris. And he was wrong.

But, of course, there was nobody on camera assigned to the weighty responsibility of fact-checking the fact-checker so the lie, disguised as a fact, went unresponded.

Meanwhile, Harris was not "fact-checked" at all by the moderators despite multiple false statements including:

- Harris claimed Trump called neo-Nazis in Charlottesville "very fine people"
- Harris accused Trump of wanting to implement Project 2025
- Harris claimed "the Trump administration resulted in a trade deficit" that was "one of the highest we've ever seen in the history of America"
- Harris claimed that Trump "wants to be a dictator on day one"
- Harris blamed her and Biden's disastrous Afghanistan withdrawal on Trump

In fact, Breitbart News cataloged 21 falsehoods uttered by Harris at the debate. Not one of her assertions was corrected or fact-checked by Muir or Davis.

The behavior of the "moderators" at CBS News during the vice presidential debate was just as bad. Despite an agreement that the tag team of O'Donnell and Brennan would not actively engage in "fact-checking" as Muir had done, Brennan couldn't help herself during one exchange over border policy.

J.D. Vance had answered a question regarding the current border security problems and he had referenced the problems that had emerged with Haitian nationals living in Springfield, Ohio.

BRENNAN: Thank you, Governor. And just to clarify for our viewers, Springfield, Ohio does have a large number of Haitian migrants who have legal status. Temporary protected status. Norah.

VANCE: Well, Margaret, Margaret, I think it's important because…

BRENNAN: Thank you, senator. We have so much to get to.

O'DONNELL: We're going to turn now to the economy. Thank you.

VANCE: Margaret. The rules were that you guys weren't going to fact-check, and since you're fact-checking me, I think it's important to say what's actually going on. So there's an application called the CBP One app where you can go on as an illegal migrant, apply for asylum or apply for parole and be granted legal status at the wave of a Kamala Harris open border wand. That is not a person coming in, applying for a green card, and waiting for ten years.

BRENNAN: Thank you, Senator.

VANCE: That is the facilitation of illegal immigration, Margaret, by our own leadership. And Kamala Harris opened up that pathway.

BRENNAN: Thank you, Senator, for describing the legal process. We have so much to get to.

WALZ: Those laws have been in the book since 1990.

BRENNAN: Thank you, gentlemen. We want to have -

VANCE: The CBP app has not been on the books since 1990. It's something that Kamala Harris created, Margaret.

BRENNAN: Gentlemen, the audience can't hear you because your mics are cut. We have so much we want to get to. Thank you for explaining the legal process. Norah?

Once again, just like Muir at ABC News, Brennan felt the need to exercise some level of power over the proceedings and to "protect" the viewers from some sort of "wrong-think" from Vance. The tone of her statement gave the impression that Vance had in some way tried to mislead in his description of the Haitians living in his state. Then, when Vance gave important and thoughtful, factual context to the proceedings and informed the viewers exactly how the definition of "legal status" had been dumbed-down and re-defined by the Biden/Harris Administration, she waved the back of her hand with a dismissive, "Thank you, Senator, for describing the legal process."

Vance was right and he corrected Brennan's not-so-veiled effort to make it seem as though Vance had lied. More importantly though, what happened in the exchange above is the fundamental problem with these so-called debates in the first place.

These two men, who are vying to lead our nation at the highest level, began an exchange over a critically important issue - perhaps one of the top issues facing voters. They began to engage in a factual and energetic exchange over refugee/asylum policies and the use of the controversial "CBP app" which has been exploited by false asylum seekers to facilitate illegal, yet protected, entry into the country. Viewers were able to watch these two men go at it and engage each other on this important topic until they were interrupted by the CBS journalists. More than interrupted, the CBS News employees used their powerful mute button to turn off their microphones so viewers couldn't hear them. Instead, the network employees decided that enough was enough on that topic and they would have to move on so Norah O'Donnell could ask her prepared question.

In other words, an actual *debate* began and it was cut off by the teleprompter readers so they could direct a *pretend* debate that isn't really a debate at all. The debate moderators took over and stopped the debate so they could get back to the script they had prepared. How is this serving the electoral process?

Although the highly-politicized "non-partisan" Presidential Debate Commission had already been rendered irrelevant by Trump with his insistence to bypass them and work directly with the networks, there was still one holdover from that regime that influenced the final, lamentable display we all witnessed: The use of network media figures as the so-called moderators.

For some reason, over the past several decades, it was determined by some unknown star-chamber that the only Americans capable of moderating a presidential debate were people whose sole skill-set boiled down to looking good on television and being able to effectively read a teleprompter.

How did this ever happen?

What about David Muir's education, work experience, life experience or professional career made him uniquely qualified to be the man who determined what questions to ask the two people poised to be President of the United States? Does he or O'Donnell bring some special knowledge or skill to this arena that couldn't also be replicated by, say, a panel of judges chosen from various parts of the country? Or, perhaps, small business owners? Or corporate CEOs? Or stay-at-home, homeschool moms? Or professional athletes? Seriously. Why are network news anchors in any way more qualified to directly ask our candidates questions than any other American citizen?

They are not.

Let's face it. These "debates" have turned into showcases for the network talent to have their "big moment" on a world stage. The incentives are there for them to make the most of that moment to further enrich their employers by bringing attention to their corporate brand, as well as to further enrich themselves by becoming "stars" who just "spoke truth to power" against the Republican candidate.

In 2012 Candy Crowley of CNN famously weighed in and falsely claimed Barack Obama had called the raid on the Benghazi consulate a terror attack when, in fact, he hadn't. It was during a particularly heated moment when Republican Mitt Romney was emphasizing Obama's laissez-faire attitude toward the September 11, attacks and the fact that Obama refused to call the terror attack a terror attack. Obama pleaded for help from Crowley and he got it.

OBAMA: Secretary Clinton has done an extraordinary job. But she works for me. I'm the president and I'm always responsible, and that's why nobody's more interested in finding out exactly what happened than I do.

The day after the attack, governor, I stood in the Rose Garden and I told the American people in the world that we are going to find out exactly what happened. That this was an act of terror and I also said that we're going to hunt down those who committed this crime.

And then a few days later, I was there greeting the caskets coming into Andrews Air Force Base and grieving with the families.

And the suggestion that anybody in my team, whether the Secretary of State, our U.N. Ambassador, anybody on my team would play politics or mislead when we've lost four of our own, governor, is offensive. That's not what we do. That's not what I do as president, that's not what I do as Commander in Chief.

ROMNEY: I — I think interesting the president just said something which — which is that on the day after the attack he went into the Rose Garden and said that this was an act of terror.

OBAMA: That's what I said.

ROMNEY: You said in the Rose Garden the day after the attack, it was an act of terror. It was not a spontaneous demonstration, is that what you're saying?

OBAMA: Please proceed governor.

ROMNEY: I want to make sure we get that for the record because it took the president 14 days before he called the attack in Benghazi an act of terror.

OBAMA: Get the transcript.

CROWLEY: It — it — it — he did in fact, sir. So let me — let me call it an act of terror...

OBAMA: Can you say that a little louder, Candy?

CROWLEY: He — he did call it an act of terror. It did as well take — it did as well take two weeks or so for the whole idea there being a riot out there about this tape to come out. You are correct about that.

Obama's skin was saved, Romney was thrown off-guard because he didn't have a Trump-like fighting spirit to press the issue, (after all, he didn't want to make anybody at CNN mad, did he?) and before you know it, the debate and the election was lost. Crowley became a short-lived "star of the moment" and was celebrated by the legacy media for doing her duty and helping their guy.

In 2020, Kristen Welker was a "rising star" for NBC News. She was chosen to moderate the final debate between Trump and Biden. The media response to her performance basically secured her superstar status and launched her into the host seat for NBC News's *Meet The Press* three years later.

As long as networks see these debates as opportunities to get attention and as long as the teleprompter readers see the high-profile affairs as tickets to fame and bigger contracts, the incentive will always exist to create a "big moment" rather than to get out of the way and let the candidates talk.

So why do we allow this to continue?

Can 2024 be the last year we cede this vital and influential job to a good haircut at a broadcast network? Why can't we open this job up to people of other professions? Why should "journalists," who overwhelmingly vote for Democrats over Republicans, be chosen for a job that, by definition, is supposed to be unbiased, fair, and moderate?

Let's choose some people from other walks of life to fill this vital role. Or, even better, let's do away with the "moderator" job altogether. Let's face it, these things aren't *really* debates at all, are they?

The typical presidential or vice-presidential debate format boils down to this:

- Fake, biased moderator asks one candidate a slanted, biased question.
- Candidate has two minutes to answer.
- Other candidate has one minute to respond.
- Candidates sometimes interrupt and challenge each other in a form of dialogue that begins to actually

resemble something any normal person would call a "debate" and suddenly...
- Fake, biased moderator steps in. Cuts-off microphones. Scolds the candidates (and the audience for being human and reacting) and then makes some comment that generally is interpreted as the moderator taking the Democrat candidate's side, because, well, they did.

That's not a debate. The moment the made-for-TV podium show *actually* starts to take on the characteristics of a debate, everything is stopped because, well, we can't have the two people who want to lead the free world *actually* engage in any kind of back-and-forth with each other... We need the teleprompter reader to intervene!

What the heck are we doing here? Why is this third person even necessary?

How about this:

- The two candidates are charged with crafting ten questions for their opponent.
- They take turns asking each other their questions and they use ten minutes for each question to engage each other in debate until the time is up.

- If the candidates are rude and bully each other and come across as jerks, the voters will see that and take it into account.

And, that's it. That's the entirety of the new debate format. Ten, ten-minute segments where each candidate asks their opponent a question and they debate each other. They monitor their own time and they monitor their own behavior.

That's it.

If a candidate and their campaign team are incapable of asking their opponent a challenging and probing question, they have no business running for the office in the first place. If they are not capable of standing on stage and having a free-wheeling discussion about the most important topics facing our country, ditto.

Whether we adopt something as radical as my "no moderator" debate format, or if we choose people from other professions beyond "network news anchor" to act in the moderator role, our nation will be better off and our voters will be better informed if we leave this old "debate" model in the ash bin of history where it belongs.

Chapter Twelve - Morning Joke: The Joe and Mika Show

MSNBC's morning show, *Morning Joe*, starring former Republican congressman Joe Scarborough and his new wife, Mika Brzezinski, is the textbook example of elitist, "smart set" political programming. The cable news mainstay is "must-see" television on the upper West and East Side of Manhattan, Chevy Chase, Bethesda, and Northwest DC. (outside those regions, the ratings are less than impressive, and MSNBC doesn't really care). The show represents mainstream liberal thought in modern Democratic Party circles and their interviews, roundtables, and monologues/rants become the morning caffeine fix for progressive urbanites who love to pretend to be informed, despite actually dwelling in a news and opinion vacuum.

Everything about the show is pretense and facade, right down to the set and broadcast facilities. Joe and Mika (as their devotees refer to them) appear in a snazzy studio setting with an image of the White House behind them as if it were right outside a big picture window. Of course, they aren't *actually* broadcasting from Lafayette Square in Washington DC, it's a giant video screen simulating a window overlooking the executive mansion. That sort of imagery is expected for shows originating from DC, but Joe and Mika take it one step further. Several steps further. To be precise: 975 miles worth of steps.

As my colleague, radio host Chris Plante first pointed out, Joe and Mika's set is a home studio located not in DC or even New York, but in Jupiter, Florida where they live and enjoy the safety and protection of a conservative Republican governor and a growing MAGA population. The fake background of Washington DC is the perfect example of the inherent phoniness of the two hosts and the entire premise of the construct they've been able to prop up as the "conscience of the American Democrat." Since Trump won the presidency in 2016, they've positioned themselves and their show as the way to start your day with a morning dose of Trump Derangement Syndrome. Never mind the fact that during the 2016 campaign, Trump appeared as a guest on the show 41 times.

Most of those appearances were during the primaries and the team cynically bolstered Trump to help his persona and his political prospects so that he could secure the nomination. The unspoken strategy was Trump is unelectable in a general election so if they could prop him up and secure the GOP nomination, their candidate of choice, Hillary Clinton, would have an easier time in November. Of course, that didn't work out well for them or Clinton.

To fend off accusations that they had been "soft" on Trump and "normalized" him, the pair began an all-out Jihad against the newly elected president. Their show became the clearing house for Russian Collusion Hoax content and every new fake Trump outrage that fueled the news cycle from 2017-2020.

As the 2024 election approached, Scarborough became increasingly shrill and outrageous in his criticisms and attacks against Trump. Scarborough described Trump as "out of his mind scared" amid legal threats, including potential criminal charges in New York. He specifically highlighted Trump's social media posts threatening riots that could lead to "death and destruction" if charged with a misdemeanor. This was in response to Trump's actions and statements around his possible indictment, where Scarborough accused Trump of "threatening violence against a prosecutor and trying to get other people to commit acts of violence." Scarborough accused Trump of "going full Nazi...full fascist" in his criticisms of Manhattan District Attorney Alvin Bragg. He claimed Trump was employing tactics reminiscent of fascist propaganda by calling Bragg an "animal" and engaging in what Scarborough described as "the whole Jewish international banker thing."

Scarborough frequently discussed how Trump's influence was affecting the Republican Party and its supporters. He criticized evangelicals supporting Trump by implying that they were backing someone described by a judge as a "rapist," highlighting a perceived moral inconsistency. He also spoke about a "sickness" among Trump supporters, suggesting that there was an unhealthy attraction to authoritarianism and totalitarianism within the party, particularly in relation to Trump's potential return to power.

He warned that a second Trump administration would undermine the Department of Justice, the FBI, and the rule of law, potentially leading to the destruction of "Madisonian democracy." Scarborough painted a picture of a dystopian future where Trump's leadership could lead to the imprisonment or execution of political adversaries, based on his interpretation of Trump's rhetoric and actions. On November 21, 2023, Scarborough warned on *Morning Joe* that Trump was, "running to end American democracy as we know it," and described him as an authoritarian. On October 23, 2023 Joe and Mika said that Trump would "wipe out" democracy if elected again, comparing Trump's potential actions to those of Hungarian Prime Minister Viktor Orban.

As vitriolic *Morning Joe* had become in its constant attacks on Trump, it was equally sycophantic when it came to bolstering and propping up Joe Biden, especially when faced with news reports focusing on his mental and cognitive decline. When the Wall Street Journal published the article "Behind Closed Doors, Biden Shows Signs of Slipping" in Spring, 2024 (see Chapter 5), Scarborough took the publication and the sources in the article to task:

There's such a, there's such a challenge for the Biden team. Because, as I've said here on the show over the past couple -- I've spent a good bit of time with Joe Biden. I've spent a couple of hours with Joe Biden, sitting, talking, going around the world as far as talking issues, talking the economy, talking inflation, talking.

And I must say, when I was talking to him, my thought wasn't, oh, poor guy. My thought was, oh, my God, I wish Dr. Brzezinski were on the other side of the table right now, cause these two guys -- I mean, 50 years of experience, and Joe Biden hasn't forgotten it. He may get pissed off at a press conference, and he may be thinking about the Mexican border deal and say Mexico instead of Egypt. He knows what he's talking about, he circles back around, gets to Egypt. He might misplace a word here or there.

But you talk to him for hours at a time. Is he slower? Does he move slower? Yeah, he moves slower. Is he stiffer? Yeah, he moves stiffer. Does he have trouble walking sometimes? Yeah, so did FDR. We get out of the Depression, we won a

G.D. war against, against Nazism and, and, and against the Japanese.

But comparing that guy's mental state -- I've said it for years now: he's cogent. But I undersold him when I said he was cogent. He's far beyond cogent. In fact, I think he's better than he's ever been intellectually, analytically. Because he's been around for 50 years and, you know, I don't know if people know this or not, Biden used to be a hot head. Sometimes that Irishman would get in front of the reasoning. Sometimes he would say things he didn't want to say. This is -- and, and, I don't -- you know what? I don't really care.

Start your tape right now, because I'm about to tell you the truth. And f-you if you can't handle the truth. This version of Biden intellectually, analytically, is the best Biden ever. Not a close second. And I've known him for years. The Brzezinskis (Scarborough's in-laws) have known him for 50 years. If it weren't the truth, I wouldn't say it.

That monologue on MSNBC the morning of March 6, became the stuff of legend, especially after Biden was forced to step down from the ticket just four and a half months later. The day after Biden's disastrous debate (see Chapter 5) Joe and Mika were in full panic mode with both of them showing themselves to be the advocates and activists - not journalists - that they clearly were.

Regular guest Mike Barnicle described the scene from the night before and tried his best to go on the offensive against Trump. "You saw Donald Trump for fully an hour and a half lying about every single issue that impacts people's lives," Barnicle said. "Lying about abortion, lying-lying about taxes, lying about the economy – just full-blown lies. Unfortunately, last night, President Biden let every fastball hanging out over the plate go by as a strike for Donald Trump. That's an indication he was just not up to it last night."

Mika immediately had to jump in and defend the president.

"Okay, okay – hold on a second," Brzezinski said. "I agree with everything you said except for the last part of it. Everybody, calm down. I'll tell you why. I mean, it's fine to not spin what happened last night, and we're not going to. He had a terrible night."

Hubby Joe didn't like the tone of his little lady so he had to jump in and defend himself and Barnicle. "By the way, Mika, everyone is calm here," Scarborough said. "You're the only one raising your voice, everybody is calm here."

"But, again, it's the 'let's just immediately pull this, let's end this, let's find someone else,'" Brzezinski said. "That attitude toward this is what I am saying slow down on," she said. "Because, again, there's no spinning it, but let's be balanced.

Let's for once show some balance in a media world that is so shrill with imbalance that we've become used to this."

"First of all, we show balance," Scarborough replied. "Second, no one is panicking. I said these were questions Joe Biden and Democrats need to ask themselves. Mike (Barnicle) said he missed one pitch down the middle after another and wasn't up to it last night, right, okay. Wasn't up to it last night. He said last night, so I will say, it's not panic. I mean, it's not being panicked. Understand what's at stake in this election, understand the window is closing very quickly. If Joe Biden is not up to doing this, and if last night did not reveal that to you and other Democrats, then it needs to be revealed pretty soon."

The best part of that hilarious exchange is, of course, the "we show balance" assertion from Joe. Yeah... balance.

Despite the attempts to salvage Biden's prospects, he was eventually forced to step aside (see chapter 7) and the pivot to Kamala Harris was distinct and definitive on *Morning Joe*.

On July 22, the Monday after Biden withdrew, Mika used the MSNBC airwaves to deliver a pep talk to the troops and begged her party to rally around Kamala Harris.

"Well, obviously, on many levels, I'm really sad. Joe Biden is a patriot. I love him. I love his family. And I love what he's done for the country. He had authenticity and touch. Whether you saw it or not, but everything about him, even sometimes the stuff. In the bumbling was part of the touch, part of the sort of empathic, very loving, very clear-eyed touch that he had that allowed him and enabled him to be an effective president. But all of that turned against him after the debate for all the reasons that we discussed. And he would say, No time to complain about it. Let's move on. It's go time.

And Democrats really have a moment of momentum here, and my hope is that they grab it and run with it, get unified, get organized, get coordinated. No more infighting. Donald Trump is not easy to beat. Not easy to beat and anyone who thinks he is back at 2016 when they're laughing at the concept. And you can see how quickly. They tried to steal the unity narrative.

And I've heard from inside Republican circles and right-wing media that the hate campaign against Kamala Harris has begun. You'll notice they purposefully pronounce her name wrong. They say KaMAHla. They do it all the time. It is on purpose. Talk is to start that hate campaign and get it going and start it churning. My hope is that major Democrats and major Republicans, from the Obamas to the Bush family, to military leaders. Get behind the democracy ticket and we move on."

There was no looking back after months and months of gaslighting about Biden's health and mental capacity. After shrill declarations that "this version of Biden intellectually, analytically, is the best Biden ever" and after defending and propping Biden up right up until the last moment, they immediately shifted and threw all their energy behind Harris. Why? Because Trump had to be stopped. Democracy was on the ticket. They couldn't let the totalitarian fascist win. The stakes were too high.

Right up until election day, the MSNBC audience was greeted every morning with a healthy dose of warnings over the pending fascist take-over of the country and the end of Democracy as we know it, or something like that. They were told this could very well be our last free election and we were warned that the Orange Hitler would take away the rights of women, immigrants, and even journalists in his never-ending violent quest for total power over our lives. And then, Trump won. And something extraordinary happened.

On Monday, November 18, less than two weeks after the election, Joe and Mika revealed to their liberal fans that they had visited *Hitler* over the weekend in Mar-a-Lago.

"Joe and I went to Mar-a-Lago, to meet personally with president-elect Trump," Brzezinski said. "It was the first time we have seen him in seven years."

"It's going to come as no surprise to anybody who watches this show, has watched it over the past year or over the past decade that we didn't see eye to eye on a lot of issues and we told him so," Scarborough said.

"What we did agree on was to restart communications," Brzezinski said. "In this meeting, President Trump was cheerful. He was upbeat. He seemed interested in finding common ground with Democrats on some of the most divisive issues, and for those asking why we would go speak to the president-elect during such fraught times—especially between us—I guess I would ask back, why wouldn't we?"

The reaction was immediate, volatile, and devastating for the morning duo. The "smart set" was not amused.

"BREAKING NEWS: I TOLD YOU SO Joe and Mika - Trump collaborators Not a word Mr. and Mrs. Vichy Quisling say can ever be trusted again - not that those words ever should have been trusted. They are confidence tricksters - and grifters" - Keith Olbermann

"Given Morning Joe and Mika are now sucking up to Trump I wanted to re-share my clip from MSNBC on Friday when I made it clear WE will NEVER surrender to Trump. We will take the fight to him. We will not meet him halfway on his fascism. We know who he is and more importantly, we know who we are" - Dean Obeidallah

"Joe and Mika going down there might be my favorite — when they had to go out there and go, 'and so we did.' Like, they spent the year going, 'this man will destroy all that you hold dear, he is a Hitler-Mussolini cocktail mix and we must all stand.' Literally one week later they're like, 'so we go and we have lunch, a light lunch. I get the watercress salad and you know Joey,'" - Jon Stewart

"So Mika and Joe went down to Mar-a-Lago to kiss the ring. It's the last time I ever watch Morning Joe. Period. End of statement. Unreal. Unreal. For months, you were telling us he's the worst thing that could happen to this country and democracy, and then you go kiss his ring? Despicable. Despicable you, both of you." - Rosie O'Donnell

Oh, you hate to see it. But, it's understandable, right? After years of warning that Trump was an evil monster, how do you go have brunch with an evil monster and pretend it's OK? Their sycophants on the left had a point and they were right to point out the hypocrisy.

The fact is, Joe and Mika had lied to their audience for all these years. They lied about how bad Trump was and lied about how good Biden was. They lied about Biden's health until they couldn't lie anymore and then immediately changed the subject in support of Harris.

Their audience felt betrayed because their audience had been lied to, on a news program, on a cable news network. It was a betrayal they wouldn't soon get over. The Joe and Mika drama perfectly illustrates the powerful, well-funded, and influential propaganda media techniques that were used against Trump over the past eight years right up through his triumphant victory on election day. Trump's victory was decisive and historic against Biden and Harris, yes. But it was also historic against the legacy media.

Joe and Mika personify that victory.

They were the worst of the worst and they targeted Trump with lies, hysteria, and hyperbole while being celebrated in the corridors of the elite institutions of political and cultural power in America. The more vitriol they threw at Trump, the more they were embraced by our nation's "smart set." Then, it was all exposed as the fraud that it was. They were wrong. They were defeated. And they went crawling to Trump to kiss the ring.

It was beautiful and it represented Trump's total victory against the media. Going forward, there are new rules that President Trump has set for American politics and the fourth estate.

Part 3 - New Rules

"The difference between you and me is that they had to change the rules so I couldn't dominate. They changed the rules for you so that you could dominate." - Wilt Chamberlin to Michael Jordan

Chapter Thirteen - Trump Defeats Them All: The Victory Over the Media

As we've explained, the "rules" or "norms" of American politics were systematically upended over the past several years to stop one man from winning (or even running) for political office.

"The norms had to be changed to stop Trump because Trump was such a threat to the norms," we were told without a shred of self-aware irony. From double impeachments that were doomed from the moment they were delivered to the Republican-led Senate, to RICO charges brought by a now-disgraced Fulton County District Attorney, to the invention of new, unfair, and unexplainable laws regarding non-disclosure agreements and campaign finance invented by a hapless District Attorney in Manhattan - Trump had to be stopped. No, Trump had to be *incarcerated*.

The explosion of "norms" went well beyond the nefarious use of "lawfare" to incarcerate but also to politically *incapacitate* a former president. The 14th Amendment of the Constitution was creatively re-interpreted to block Trump from even *appearing* on ballots in Colorado, Michigan, Maine and potentially even more states had the Supreme Court not flushed those bogus attempts down the judicial toilet. Democrats attempted political and legal assassinations of Trump whenever possible and none of their attempts could have been possible if they didn't know they'd have compliant (if not active and willing) partners in the legacy media. From the networks to the cable news outlets, to major newspapers and websites, basic journalistic "norms" were upended and discarded as political media willingly turned themselves into nothing more than propaganda machines to aid and fully participate in the unprecedented attack on Trump and the democratic process. The media was more than willing to use their resources to end Trump's political chances and cheer on the attempts to keep him off the ballot, thus keeping the American people from even having the opportunity to vote for the candidate of their choice. But, a funny thing happened on the way to the gulag... Trump didn't quit. He fought back ten times harder.

And he won.

Despite the Democrats and the propagandist media's efforts to disqualify Trump from the ballot, from office, and from polite society - when the American people had the chance to have their say, they overwhelmingly said "We want this man back in the White House." He won in every "battleground" state (he only needed to win a majority of them). He won the Electoral College vote by a wider margin than his 2016 victory. He even won the "popular vote" - which is not actually a real thing since the President of the United States is not elected by popular vote but by the Electoral College - but he won that too!

He won in the most meaningful way a person in American politics can win. We won at the ballot box, by the will of the American people.

But, what if I told you that his victory over Kamala Harris (and Joe Biden four months prior) was not his most significant victory? What if I told you that Trump's most impactful win - his legacy - is his victory over those very propagandists who worked to defeat him on Biden and Harris' behalf?

Hear me out:

Winning the presidency is huge, no doubt. To further his agenda through lasting legislation and executive action, only electoral victory and four years in the Oval Office would suffice. Clearly, Trump as the CEO of the Executive Branch of the Federal Government will be impactful and historic during his second term. His victory over the media, however, will be historic in its own right, and, I would argue, that Trump is *literally* the only man in history who could've carried it off. Every politician before Trump would've "played by the rules" when it comes to the media. They would've listened to their high-paid consultants and they would've done what they could to accommodate the "powerful" news anchors, *New York Times* reporters and *60 Minutes* producers. Every politician before Trump would buy into the myth that if they just played along and accommodated the DC/NYC media megalopoly then they'd get a fair shake. They'd be treated tough, but fair from reporters who were, after all, just doing their jobs.

Not Trump. Trump knew better. He'd tried that game and he saw how it would end. Also, Trump knew how the media worked. He was, after all, one of them.

He was one of the most successful stars of NBC's primetime line-up. He knew the players, from the boardroom to the gaffers and cameramen in the studio. (The latter all overwhelmingly love him, by the way… Just ask them next time you're about to do an appearance on MSNBC - as I have.) He knew their business and he knew how things were done. He not only knew how the media *worked*, but he knew how to *work* the media.

Work the media he did- and he defeated them all.

As we detailed in Part 2 of this book, he defeated every attempt to shamelessly lie about him and about his opponents. He defeated the media's attempt to lie about the Biden record on the economy, national security, border security, and foreign affairs. He defeated the media's attempt to cover up Biden's mental and physical decline.

He defeated the media's attempt to cover up the Democrats' coup when they removed Biden from the ticket and crowned Kamala without so much as a vote cast on her behalf by a single Democrat. He defeated their attempts to memory-hole the attempt on his life and any scrutiny of the would-be assassin. He defeated their lies about Charlottesville, about his "bloodbath" comment, and his "Dictator on Day One" joke. He defeated their attempt to stage a scripted reality show and pretend that it was a political debate.

He defeated all of their attempts to destroy him. He defeated them all.

Indeed, one of the most significant victories he enjoyed over his enemies in the legacy media was a self-inflicted forfeiture the media willingly and stupidly engaged in. You could say, the media defeated themselves on this one. They forfeited their last gasp of credibility by consistently overreaching in their vitriolic attacks on Donald J. Trump.

Their desperate attempts to paint Trump as a fascist - nay, as Hitler reincarnate - rendered their influence and credibility practically null. They constantly referred to Trump as an insurrectionist, rapist, and felon. When the American people were able to learn exactly what the details behind these accusations were, they realized that Trump may have acted boorish or obnoxious or even offensive, but he wasn't any of the things the media claimed he was. Not by the American people's perception, at least.

Viewers, readers, and listeners were able to sift through the accusations, see the reality, and reach their conclusions. This scenario then led them to ask themselves a very reasonable question: If this network or cable station or newspaper is lying to me about this, what else are they lying about? Why should I trust anything they say?

This climate came directly after the hysteria over the COVID-19 pandemic, where the mainstream media was exposed along with public health institutions and elected officials as over-stating, over-hyping, or outright lying about the dangers we faced or the precautions we were forced to adopt. This one-two punch of misinformation became the death knell of the legacy media as we know it.

The most significant evidence of the lack of credibility and influence of these mainstream outlets came in the precipitous and drastic decline in viewership for two of the major channels peddling the propaganda against Trump: CNN and MSNBC. MSNBC saw a decline of around 46% to 55% in primetime viewership compared to their pre-election averages. Specifically, MSNBC's primetime viewership fell by 53% from October's numbers to an average of 620,000 viewers. Programs like "The Rachel Maddow Show" experienced a 43% to 56% drop in viewership.

CNN's viewership also dropped significantly, with declines reported between 33% to 46%. In primetime, CNN lost about 46% of its audience, averaging 398,000 viewers in the week post-election. A stark contrast to their election night coverage where they managed to draw 5.1 million viewers.

This wasn't just a symptom of left-leaning viewers no longer wanting to follow the news. No. This was much more significant than that and it represented much more.

Not only had these outlets delivered propaganda about Trump and Vance that turned out to be ineffective or even outright deceptive, but they also were exposed for propping up Kamala Harris (and Joe Biden before her) as some kind of second coming. CNN and MSNBC viewers were fed a regular diet of "Harris and Walz are the greatest politicians of our era and they've run a perfect campaign!" And yet, the American voters disagreed. Viewers understandably reached one of two conclusions: Either these outlets were telling the truth about the Democrat ticket but they lacked any level of influence and credibility so the American voter didn't get the message and ignored the obvious truth that was laid before them by CNN and MSNBC, or, CNN and MSNBC were just flat-out wrong.

Either way, why would you continue to patronize a news outlet that was either wrong or lacked any level of influence in the most important news story they covered all year? You wouldn't. And so, the viewers left. They left in droves. And unless those outlets make significant changes, those viewers may never come back.

There was another psychological factor at play with the decline in viewership in these left-leaning cable news outlets. Their viewers felt flat-out lied to about Harris' chances of winning. Viewers believed that the hosts and analysts hadn't just gotten it all wrong, but rather viewers believed these hosts and analysts *knew* their candidates of choice were flawed and were not going to win - but they kept lying to their viewers to keep them happy and engaged. They were told, on a regular basis, that Harris had run a perfect campaign. On election night, MSNBC's Joy Reid kept the charade going.

Reid described Kamala Harris's campaign as having been run "flawlessly" and "historic." She emphasized that anyone familiar with the United States' history would understand the difficulty of electing a woman president, especially a woman of color, thereby excusing her dismal performance as yet another symptom of America's inherent racism and sexism. Wow, what a new and innovative political take for MSNBC to hold.

What was Ms. Reid's evidence of Harris' so-called "flawless" campaign?

Reid noted that she had endorsements from prominent celebrities like Queen Latifah, Taylor Swift's "Swifties," and Beyoncé's "BeyHive," suggesting that these endorsements were indicative of a well-run, "flawless" campaign. Yes, the expert analysis from MSNBC's prime-time host was that Kamala Harris ran a flawless campaign because she was endorsed by celebrities. I think it's fair to say that the average MSNBC viewer is more in tune with politics than Ms. Reid if the best she can come up with is "celebrity endorsements" as evidence. That's especially true considering that pretty much every single Democrat running for president going back to Jack Kennedy has received the lion's share of celebrity endorsements out of Hollywood.

I'm sorry that Ms. Reid doesn't recognize that, but I assure you, her viewers do. And it's perfectly fair for those viewers to conclude that Ms. Reid is about as sharp as a bowling ball, or she's just outright lying.

Either way, why keep rewarding such stupidity or blatant mendacity, especially when there are so many alternative places to get smart and truthful news and analysis? Never again will the "experts" on TV be believed without question. Never again will the teleprompter readers be trusted "just because." Never again will these outlets enjoy the benefit of the doubt.

And we are all better off for it. Sorry, not sorry.

These are the benefits of Trump's victories over the media. In fact, Trump's victories in November of 2024 were victories over the old, broken way the legacy media did their dirty business in the first place and it signaled the opportunity for new rules to be employed going forward.

These are the new rules Republicans will employ when running for office and when messaging their agenda to the American people if they are smart enough to use these rules. Republicans don't need to play the stupid, slanted game the media created to set them up for failure. Trump has shown the way.

Republicans in Florida and Texas utilized their legislative majorities and passed laws aiming to limit how tech companies moderate content. These new laws were responses to the obvious and blatant bias against conservative viewpoints that were "moderated out" of their platforms by the overwhelming left-wing executives at those companies. The laws were sent back to lower courts by the Supreme Court for further analysis under the First Amendment, but any level of legal push-back that survives constitutional scrutiny will be welcome relief and other states should follow suit.

The new rules also applied to Republicans' need or obligation to play on the national, New York/DC dominated media playground at all. Republicans can now virtually ignore national media outlets, unless that outlet makes a legitimate effort to treat them fairly and to show scrutiny of their Democrat rivals. Republicans would be wiser to just focus on local media outlets (who tend to be more balanced and in touch with the values of their local viewers) and avoid the networks and the DC/NYC papers.

Republicans can also go directly to talk radio or the multiple streaming platforms that offer smart, live, unedited, long-form interviews where they get a fairer opportunity to show themselves and deliver their message. We'll explore Republicans' opportunities to bypass the traditional, legacy gatekeepers in the next chapter, but make no mistake, these are the most significant new rules for GOP lawmakers across the country. And the rules all stem from Trump's victories. "To the winner goes the spoils." In this case, the spoils would be the ability to direct how things will go from this point forward. Trump did that.

And we all owe him a huge debt of gratitude -if we're all wise enough to take advantage of these spoils. We should all be wise enough to follow through and officially, once and for all, ignore the dominance that mainstream outlets have given themselves, without any actual merit. The reality is that the legacy media emperor has no clothes.

"Mainstream" media is not mainstream at all. They do not represent the mainstream in this country, ideologically or geographically. Why should a morning news show on a fringe cable station that only has any significant viewership in Manhattan and DC be considered "mainstream"? Joe and Mika and the clown car that populates the roundtable on MSNBC's *Morning Joe* are somehow called "mainstream media" Why?

The topics and perspectives put forth on the show certainly bear no resemblance to the politics or ideologies of mainstream Americans. The Manhattan-based Network (with Joe and Mika famously phoning it in from their garage studio in Florida, designed to appear as though they're in

Washington DC) certainly has nothing to do with mainstream America in any real, geographic sense. MSNBC's Joe and Mika show is anything but "mainstream" and the American people recognize that. That emperor is nude as all get out!

The same can be said for network news with David Muir, Lester Holt, and Nora O'Donnell. Ditto the Sunday shows with George Stephanopoulos, Kristen Welker, and Margaret Brennan.

So why must we play along with this farce? Why continue to call them "mainstream media" when in no way other than legacy are they representatives of the mainstream of America?

We shouldn't.

We should call them what they are: Propaganda. Propaganda on behalf of their corporate ownership (Disney, Comcast, Viacom, etc.) and propaganda on behalf of their party, the Democrats. They are nothing more than that. Trump's overwhelming victory against them and their constant, relentless propaganda efforts against him has finally exposed their true nature for all to see.

That is if anyone's still watching.

Chapter Fourteen - The Podcast Election: Bypassing the Gatekeepers

To say that Trump's appearance on the Joe Rogan podcast was a significant and game-changing moment in the 2024 presidential election is hardly groundbreaking or insightful. It's rather obvious. But, if I may, the reason this moment was so significant has been lost on not a small number of observers.

As a purely political strategic maneuver, it was brilliant. He agreed to sit for the interview less than two weeks before election day. With so little time left, it boxed the Harris campaign in.

Rogan immediately expressed his interest in securing the Democratic nominee for an interview and Harris had a decision to make. Does she snub the most popular podcaster/influencer on the planet? Does she show up for a no-hold-barred, free-wheeling, three-hour conversation where she will have no place to hide and will be pressed with tough follow-up questions (something she only experienced once in a less-than-twenty-minute sit down with Fox News' Bret Baier)? Or, does she claim she really wanted to do the interview but then offer a lame excuse that nobody would believe?

Naturally, she chose option three.

In a post-election appearance on the lefty podcast *Pod Save America*, Harris campaign insider Stephanie Cutter claimed that negotiations to get Harris on the Rogan show had been ongoing, but to make the trek to the studios in Austin, Texas (where Rogan insisted the interviews take place) would've meant taking her candidate off the campaign trail of a battleground state.

The geniuses running Harris's campaign decided it wasn't worth the gamble.

"There's a lot of intrigue around this, a lot of theories, it's pretty simple. We wanted to do it. I hate to repeat this over and over, but it was a very short race with a limited number of days and for a candidate to leave the battleground to go to Houston, which is a day off the playing field in the battleground, getting that timing right is really important. So we had discussions with Joe Rogan's team, they were great, they wanted us to come on, we wanted to come on, we tried to get a date to make it work and ultimately we just weren't able to find a date. We did go to Houston and she gave a great speech at an amazing event."

Now, far be it for me to suggest that a well-respected Democrat campaign operative like Cutter, a veteran of ObamaLand and ClintonWorld, would fabricate a self-serving lie to save face and save her client's political reputation, but this doesn't pass the smell test. First of all, Cutter seems completely unfamiliar with the details of the Rogan show as she continues to refer to the studio location as Houston rather than Austin. Second, if pulling your candidate off of the trail of a battleground state was a bad idea, then why did Trump win, because that is *exactly* what *their* campaign did?

The reality is, as everyone knows, there is no possible way she would ever have done that interview with Joe Rogan or anybody else for that matter. Kamala Harris is *literally* incapable of sitting and answering questions for three hours without revealing herself to be incompetent, incoherent, unlikeable, ill-prepared, and, worst of all, a tried and true, doctrinaire California liberal. This assessment has little to do with *Rogan's* politics, which are complicated if not indecipherable.

Yes, he endorsed Trump, but in the same way, Robert F. Kennedy Jr. endorsed him. It wasn't because they share political ideologies in a traditional liberal vs. conservative sort of way. It was more because Rogan, like Kennedy, had become so disaffected with the Democrats (their natural political home) that they concluded the only real way to fix them was to defeat them.

No, the determination that Harris was incapable of sitting with Rogan for three hours comes more from recognizing that she was incapable of sitting with the cast of *The View* for twenty minutes without causing terminal damage to her campaign. Whoopi Goldberg, Joy Bahar, and Sonny Hostin of *The View* were three women who professed undying affection for both Biden and Harris. They overtly promoted and supported their campaigns and utilized their high-profile positions on ABC News to attack Trump while defending Harris daily. The nominal "Republican" on the show's panel, Alyssa Farah Griffin, was in reality a vitriolic Never-Trump Republican-in-name-only who was as equally hostile to Trump as her liberal colleagues.

Yet even in that warm, hospitable environment, Harris delivered what may have been her single worst moment of the campaign (and that is really saying something). Hostin asked Harris what should have been the softest of softball questions. Indeed, a question she should have been more than prepared to answer.

"If anything, would you have done something differently than President Biden during the past four years?" Hostin asked.

Frankly, Harris should have been able to answer this question without any hesitation. In fact, it's a question that Harris should've asked and answered herself as she looked into her bathroom mirror the day she was deciding whether to run for president in the first place.

"Kamala," she should have asked as she applied Crest to her toothbrush, "what would you have done differently in the past three years if you had been sitting at that Resolute desk?"

If Kamala looking back at herself couldn't come up with a good answer, then she should've recognized right then and there that she had no business running for president in the first place. As it turns out, she had no answer.

After an awkward second, she said:

"There is not a thing that comes to mind in terms of — and I've been a part of most of the decisions that have had impact."

This was so devastatingly bad on multiple levels.

First, and most obviously, in a country reeling with double-digit inflation, rampant crime, a wide-open border, an active war in Eastern Europe, and Iran-backed terrorists murdering innocent Americans and Israelis in the Middle East, most Americans were in the mood to know that the next president would do one or two things differently than the current incompetent at 1600 Pennsylvania. Yet, Kamala Harris, in all her political brilliance, just let every voter know that they should expect four more years of the same if they vote for her. But this awful answer caused even more damage beyond just that.

It also echoed a similar moment in the 1980 Democratic primary between President Jimmy Carter and Senator Edward "Teddy" Kennedy. Kennedy had decided to oppose his party's incumbent president with a primary challenge. The economic situation was awful, not unlike the Biden economy 44 years later. America had also suffered humiliating moral defeats internationally with the Iran hostage crisis as well as the Soviet Union's incursion into Afghanistan.

Kennedy decided this was his chance to follow in his two older brothers' footsteps and pursue the White House. During his quixotic campaign, he was asked a similar question as Harris.

"Why do you want to be president?" Roger Mudd of CBS asked Kennedy in November of 1979. Seemingly caught off guard by such a simple question whose answer seemed so obvious that one would never have expected it to be asked in the first place, Kennedy completely and historically whiffed.

Well... I'm um... were I to... to make the uh... the announcement and uh... to run... the reasons that I would run is because I have a great belief in this country that it is... there's more natural resources than any nation of the world, has the greatest educated population in the world the greatest technology of any country in the world... uh... the greatest capacity for innovation in the world and the greatest political system in the world and yet... um... I see at the current time that uh... most of the industrial nations of the world are exceeding us in terms of productivity are doing better than us in terms of meeting the problems of inflation that they're dealing with their problems of energy and their problems of unemployment and it just seems to me that uh... this nation can cope and deal with its problems in a way that it has in the past we're facing complex issues and problems in this nation at this time but we have faced similar challenges at other times and the energies and the resourcefulness of this nation I think should be focused on these problems in a way that brings a sense of uh... restoration uh... in this country by its people to in dealing with the problems that we face primarily the issues on the economy the problems of inflation and the problems of um... uh... energy and uh... I would uh... basically uh... feel that uh... that it's imperative for this country to either move forward that, it can't stand still or otherwise it moves backward.

At that moment, Kennedy's campaign was doomed because it reinforced what most Americans assumed about his controversial challenge to Carter: That this was not based on principle or policy but more on narcissistic ambition. He was a Kennedy, after all. Why would you even *ask* why he was running for president? Isn't it obvious? I'm a Kennedy, it's what we do. It's my birthright.

And this is exactly what was inferred in Kamala's ham-handed non-answer on *The View*. She couldn't answer what she would've done differently than her predecessor because it had never even occurred to her to ponder such a question. The dirty business of policies and plans and vision for the country was for normal candidates. She was, after all, Kamala Harris.

She was Vice President. She was next in line. It was her turn. She was a woman of color. Doesn't all of this speak for itself? Why ask such a silly, irrelevant question?

Now, if Harris revealed so much incompetence, narcissism, and lack of political know-how on the friendly, low-risk set of *The View*, who on this planet thinks she could have held her own for three hours on the set of *The Joe Rogan Show*? This is why there was no possible way she was ever going to do that show. And by waiting until the final weeks of the campaign to appear, Trump boxed her in. He revealed her weakness, and furthered the ongoing narrative of the campaign that she was afraid or incapable of answering questions - and he was unafraid to go anywhere.

Now, this was the obvious reason why Trump going on Rogan was such a significant and game-changing moment. But, I promised a more nuanced reason that may have gotten lost on most observers.

To understand how Trump's decision to appear with Rogan marked such a cultural change in American politics, you must first understand Trump's other major decision in this campaign regarding his media appearances.

Weeks before his Rogan appearance, Trump announced that he would not make himself available for an interview with CBS News's *60 Minutes* unless the news program apologized for the 2020 interview and released the transcript of the interview with Kamala Harris. As we explored in chapter 9, *60 Minutes* had deceptively edited their interview with the Democrat nominee, ostensibly to make her look better than her incoherent word salad originally conveyed. They had also helped sabotage Trump four years earlier with Leslie Stahl working pro-bono for the Biden campaign (and Hunter Biden's legal defense team).

Trump had determined that *60 Minutes*, the crown jewel of serious American journalism, was garbage. He decided that he didn't need them to win the presidency. He concluded they were irrelevant.

One cannot fully appreciate Trump's decision to give Joe Rogan three hours of uninterrupted, unedited, live-to-tape access without juxtaposing the decision against his equally unprecedented rejection of *60 Minutes*. You see, you just don't do what Trump did. You just don't.

Everybody knows that if you want to be considered a legitimate presidential candidate you have to go on *60 Minutes*. Everybody knows that the *60 Minutes* interview is crucial for a campaign to be taken seriously. Everybody knows that going on *60 Minutes* is an important and ritualistic exercise that, like it or not, every candidate must submit themselves to if they're lucky enough to be invited.

And then there was Trump.

It's not like Trump was the first Republican to recognize that *60 Minutes* was ideologically hostile to every preceding GOP nominee for the past 40 years. Everybody knew that too. But everybody still played along. Trump saw what his predecessors all saw, but he had the cajónes to say "no."

Not just "no," but "HELL NO."

He said "no" and publicly exposed them as the in-the-tank, left-wing liars they've always been, but then he demonstrated he had no fear of a tough but fair interview by sitting for Rogan's marathon session. It was brilliant. And it secured the most important victory of Trump's battle against the media propagandists. It fully, finally, and decisively rendered the mainstream media gatekeepers toothless and ineffective.

We no longer live in a world where the only way voters can see their prospective candidates for president answer questions that matter to them is to tune in to a cable news or broadcast network. We no longer have to hope that Leslie Stahl, Lester Holt or Wolf Blitzer ask the person who wants to be president a question that actually matters to us and our neighbors. We no longer need to wait for a special edition of the *New York Times* where a candidate sits for two hours answering questions crafted by a handful of Ivy League graduates who all work and live in the same 3-mile radius in Manhattan, New York but have never visited Manhattan, Kansas.

This is a new world. A world free of gatekeepers.

Those chosen few on cable/broadcast news or the *New York Times* editorial board not only had the monopoly on quizzing the candidates, but they also had complete and total editorial control over the candidates' answers. They could determine what we the people would be allowed to see, hear, and read from these interviews. They determined how we would receive the news and information that would inform our votes. They decided what questions as well as which answers we could see. They were the gatekeepers. And Donald Trump just crashed through their gates.

In reality, the Rogan podcast was the culmination of a campaign-long strategy that emphasized new non-traditional streaming shows and podcasts that were diverse and unique but had some very significant commonalities. Most importantly, they were accessed on platforms like YouTube, Spotify, X, and Rumble that were not controlled by the same corporations that have monopolized the delivery of political news for the past several decades. They were also for the most part either live and direct to viewers or live to tape and accessed directly by viewers with the click of a link.

This meant no editing. No subterfuge. No manipulation.

It also meant that the viewers, the American voters, could determine when and how to watch the interviews and gather the information. This was all very liberating. Furthermore, it also allowed for the democratization of the analysis and commentary on the interview in a way that will forever change the political media in America.

Think about it: Up until now, these cable and broadcast shows all followed the same script. They'd present the edited interview with the candidate. The interview was often presented to make the high-paid anchor/host look fabulous and to make the candidate (especially the Republican candidate) look defensive and suspicious. Then, after the interview, the program would often shift to a "roundtable" discussion populated by "analysts" who would then give their opinions on what we all just watched.

This was the networks' opportunity to shape public opinion by telling the viewers what they should be thinking about the candidate and the candidate's answers. More often than not, the "roundtable" was metaphorically oblong as the ideological make-up would constantly be slanted in the left-of-center direction.

Can you think of one pro-Trump analyst on any broadcast network right now? Even one? I can't, and I follow these things for a living. If CBS, NBC, or ABC are to have a "roundtable" discussion of politics right now, there is literally nobody on these networks' payrolls to speak on behalf of the majority of American voters who just chose Donald Trump. So you can imagine how these "roundtable" discussions will go. You can imagine what the analysis of the interview would consist of. The commentary on the interview, often the last word viewers would hear, would almost always be hostile to Trump.

Not so with these direct-to-viewer, streaming podcast interviews.

The full democratization of the commentary on these interviews was manifested in real-time in the very lively and entertaining comment section appearing right below the video player. No need to wait for the slanted, biased, and overpaid panel of "experts" to tell you what you should think about the interview you just saw. No. Just read and participate in the commentary and analysis in real-time right now in the comment section. You can even engage in a debate with the commenters you disagree with. This is the new media on steroids. This is what it looks like to have political content without the gatekeepers.

This is what democracy looks like, to coin a favorite lefty phrase.

Chapter Fifteen - I Stream, You Stream, We All Stream

"The medium is the message" - Marshall McLuhan, *Understanding Media: The Extensions of Man* - 1964

Marshall McLuhan's theory suggests that the *nature* of a communication *medium* inherently shapes the content and how it is perceived by the audience. In 1964, this theory was aptly applied to television, the relatively new and dominant communication of the time. The theory has certainly held up over the decades, especially when it comes to political messaging and the way Americans consume information as well as the way politicians conform their messages to accommodate the medium.

McLuhan's theory goes well beyond the RCA TV sets Americans had in their living rooms in 1964. How does "the medium is the message" extrapolate to hand-held devices streaming live video shows across the planet, delivered on social media platforms with real-time comment sections? Just look at how the streaming medium has changed the message in narrative, entertainment-based storytelling.

Streaming services like Netflix, YouTube, or Spotify change how content is consumed. By offering on-demand access, streaming has shifted viewing and listening habits from scheduled programming to personalized, anytime consumption. This medium affects the message by emphasizing personalized content, binge-watching, and the creation of content fit for streaming (e.g., shorter seasons with cliffhangers to keep viewers engaged).

The streaming medium allows for different storytelling techniques compared to traditional television or cinema. Series can have longer, more complex narratives due to the absence of commercial breaks or the need to fit into specific time slots - which influences the storytelling approach and viewer engagement. Streaming has democratized content creation and distribution, enabling a broader range of voices and stories to be shared, which in itself is part of the message – cultural democratization through the medium. When you realize that political messaging and news are now also delivered on these streaming platforms, reaching an audience already adapted to this new messaging format, you can see how streaming could have a direct influence on what people are seeing and hearing as much as how they are viewing it.

Now add the influence of social media constructs, which go hand-in-hand with the delivery systems of these streaming services. Social media platforms like X (formerly Twitter), Instagram, and TikTok enforce specific formats (e.g., character limits, video lengths, or visual emphasis) that dictate how messages are crafted and consumed. For instance, X's character limit encourages concise communication, which can affect how nuanced arguments are presented or perceived, often leading to a focus on headlines or punchy statements over detailed discourse.

The medium of social media influences user behavior by fostering environments where engagement is measured through likes, shares, and comments. This pushes creators to tailor their content for virality or quick consumption rather than depth. This can lead to a culture of instant gratification and can shape social norms around communication speed and brevity.

Social media platforms create communities and echo chambers where the medium's structure (algorithms and user interface) can amplify certain types of messages - often those that resonate with the platform's design or business model, affecting public opinion and behavior. The medium influences what becomes "common knowledge" or popular discourse. Knowing that these mediums are now the most important delivery systems for a politician's message, it's informative to recognize the ground-shaking changes we witnessed in the 2024 presidential election and how it, ultimately, paves the way for a democratized political media which tips the balance of power back to the people from the elite handful of gatekeepers we discussed in Chapter 14.

The greatest power the gatekeepers of the old media paradigm possessed and wielded was the technological platforms designed to deliver content via broadcast airwaves, cable, and Internet.

The ultimate power of controlling information flow rested in the hands of the few corporations who owned networks capable of financing the costs involved in presenting content on any one of these pipelines. Whether it was radio, television cable, or the web, only a select few would be fortunate enough to be chosen to be seen and heard by the American public for the first century of electronic media.

Now, the rules have changed.

Over the past several years, Americans began the process of "cutting the cable" on their televisions and adopting the process of choosing the apps, channels, or shows that they want. It's now delivered to their phones, laptops, and even their smart TVs via a high-speed broadband connection. Viewers left the prison of basic-cable, 100-channel packages which only offered 5-10 channels viewers actually wanted to see but charged for the other 90 channels. The consumer recognized that they would rather pay for the content they actually wanted rather than be forced into paying for content they had no interest in. If you are a conservative news junkie and love romantic movies but couldn't care less about sports or children's programming, then you could subscribe to apps that just offered the one or two news channels you prefer and the Hallmark channel, forgoing left-wing news outlets, ESPN and Nickelodeon.

As this shift started to accelerate, major networks leapt into the market with their own apps targeting the consumers who knew them best and would be most likely to subscribe directly to the content creators rather than through a cable delivery system. CBS offers Paramount+, NBC has Peacock and ABC is now streaming multitudes of content on Disney+. Disney+, quickly became the dominant streaming alternative in America thanks to Disney's early adaptation to the streaming genre (2019) and the extraordinarily diverse and vast catalog of content Disney owns. Now that content is immediately available on-demand for their subscribers.

From the entire Disney catalog going all the way back to *Steamboat Willie* to the Marvel movie franchises, to the *Star Wars* franchises, Disney-owned movies and shows and specials that they had been creating or acquiring for nearly 100 years. Throw in a pandemic lockdown that forced every human being into their living rooms for a year, and habits were quickly formed. Disney+ was poised to dominate this new medium and rise as the top provider of streaming content, including their ABC News programs, for years to come. But then, in Summer of 2024, right in the middle of the presidential election, something extraordinary happened:

"By July 2024, YouTube had become the first streaming service to exceed 10% of all TV viewing in the U.S., showing a significant increase in time spent by viewers, particularly during the summer when Disney+ content might see a dip due to seasonal programming or school holidays. This trend was highlighted in reports from sources like Nielsen, indicating YouTube's dominance in TV viewing time." - Jack Reid, Next TV

Yes, YouTube defeated Disney as the top streaming content provider. YouTube, the on-demand streaming platform that also combines community-building, and social media mechanics was now the #1 destination for individuals to receive entertainment, music, DIY instruction, *and political* content. This includes cable-produced and network-produced content, as well. The number one streaming service for network and cable television content is YouTube TV, YouTube's streaming alternative to cable or satellite content services.

YouTube TV is widely recognized for its comprehensive channel lineup, which includes major broadcast networks like ABC, CBS, NBC, and Fox, along with a broad selection of cable channels such as ESPN, CNN, and AMC. It offers unlimited DVR storage, supports 4K streaming with an add-on, and provides a user-friendly interface, making it a top choice for those looking to replace traditional cable TV. Its extensive sports coverage, including exclusive NFL games, further solidifies its position as a leading service for live TV streaming.

In short, if you were utilizing a streaming service in 2024 to consume network or cable content, you were more likely using YouTube for it. How does a streaming platform change the media and the way the presidential election was covered? How do viewing habits moving toward streaming content undermine the gatekeepers' monopoly on political content? It's best explained through the journey of one video news personality whose career has almost perfectly coincided with this dramatic shift: Megyn Kelly.

Megyn Kelly's professional journey has been notable for its transitions across different platforms in the media landscape. Megyn Kelly started her television career at Fox News, where she joined in 2004. She became a prominent figure, hosting shows like "America's Newsroom," "America Live," and eventually "The Kelly File," which became one of the highest-rated cable news programs. Her time at Fox News was marked by high-profile interactions with major political figures including with then-candidate Donald Trump during the 2016 Republican presidential debates, which garnered significant attention. Kelly was seen as relatively hostile toward Trump and Trump returned the hostility, as he does. No matter who you "blame" for the hostilities, the ratings were gold, and Kelly's star-power and value shot through the roof.

In January 2017, Kelly announced her departure from Fox News to join NBC News, citing a desire for new challenges and more family time. At NBC, she was set to host a daytime talk show, "Megyn Kelly Today," which premiered in September 2017, as well as a Sunday night newsmagazine show, "Sunday Night with Megyn Kelly." Her stint at NBC was tumultuous.

"Megyn Kelly Today" struggled with ratings, and she faced controversies, notably when she made comments defending blackface in the context of Halloween costumes in October 2018. These remarks led to significant backlash and an attempt by NBC News insiders to "cancel" the new network star. Despite an apology, "Megyn Kelly Today" was canceled two days later. Her Sunday night show did not fare well in terms of viewership either, leading to her exit from NBC in January 2019.

NBC agreed to pay Kelly the remaining sum of her three-year contract, which was worth $69 million in total. At the time of her exit, she was halfway through this contract so the remaining payment was estimated to be around $30 million. Kelly was subject to an industry-standard non-disparagement clause. This clause typically limits what she can say about her time at NBC and her interactions with NBC executives publicly, ensuring that neither party can speak negatively about the other post-departure. Importantly, Kelly was not believed to be subject to a non-compete clause, meaning she was free to join another network or start her own media venture immediately after leaving NBC. And, that's exactly what she did.

From NBC's perspective, they figured they couldn't be harmed by Kelly "going across the street" to compete with the Peacock network. After all, she was leaving under a cloud that included whispers of her unacceptable political independence. "How dare she not tow the DEI line on the black-face issue! See! She's the Fox News racist we always figured she was!" Further, NBC probably figured Fox News would never take her back, either, after her public departure. So, pay her off and she'll just disappear, NBC thought.

Kelly had other ideas. You give a talent like Kelly a $30 million bankroll to start her own venture and she'll probably end up on top. And with the new democratization of video media sweeping the world, you don't need anything near $30 million to make a splash.

After leaving NBC, Kelly did not return to traditional broadcast television. Instead, she launched "*The Megyn Kelly Show*" as a video podcast on YouTube in August 2021 and as an audio-only subscription program on SiriusXM in September 2021. This move allowed her to have full editorial control over her content.

The podcast has become one of the fastest-growing conservative talk show podcasts, showcasing her continued influence in media outside of traditional networks. Her shift to podcasting has been seen as a successful rebranding, focusing on her ability to connect with audiences through a more direct and personal medium. Kelly's career trajectory illustrates a shift from being a central figure in cable news at Fox to a challenging period at a major broadcast network like NBC and finally as an independent media personality with a strong digital presence.

The Megyn Kelly journey and her ultimate success on YouTube and digital delivery platforms perfectly demonstrates the liberation for creators like Kelly, Rogan, or Ben Shapiro, but it also tees-up the last aspect of this information democratization; the audience participation in what makes information spread and take hold in the American conscious.

As we stated, YouTube TV is now the top delivery platform for traditional media. As you're watching your favorite cable news program on a multi-million dollar set with a multi-million dollar teleprompter reader telling you how you should vote, a very interesting and valuable thing will appear on your screen. YouTube TV offers recommendations of other programming options on their platform based on viewer habits.

The service uses your watch history and recorded shows to tailor suggestions, making the viewing experience more personalized. YouTube TV also factors in what is trending or popular in your location to provide more relevant content. This includes both live programs and suggestions to add to your library. Additionally, YouTube TV shares your search and watch history across YouTube and YouTube TV, which can influence the recommendations you see on YouTube TV based on your activity on both platforms.

YouTube TV recommendations can include content from YouTube Original creators. YouTube Originals are part of the broader YouTube ecosystem, and content from these series can appear in recommendations on YouTube TV, especially if you have watched similar content or have a history of viewing YouTube Originals on either YouTube or YouTube TV. This integration helps in providing a seamless experience across both platforms, where your watch history on YouTube can influence recommendations on YouTube TV.

In other words, if you are a news junkie and frequent viewer of political news content, YouTube will begin suggesting other shows to you that fit your viewing habits and your preferences. If you start clicking on those recommendations, you are bound to get more refined and custom recommendations in your news feed and soon your channel options will be more customized for your interests and preferences. This means you'll start seeing independent content creators that you may never have heard of being recommended to you based on your previous viewing habits.

 Megyn Kelly, sitting at a desk and talking straight into a camera is now recommended to you because you watched a cable news program. And because you watched Megyn Kelly, you'll now get a recommendation of a person talking into their camera that might not be as famous as Kelly, but the content may be even more to your liking. These recommendations now end up helping you form your viewing habits, but it also helps that person talking into the camera attached to their computer build an audience and revenue for their production.

Before you know it, you're part of a vast audience of viewers who are helping to move political content that otherwise may never have been seen before. This allows individuals with relatively meager means to actually build a large and influential following by providing analysis and perspective - individuals the gatekeepers at the networks would never have even allowed into their offices. More to the point, a large number of the audience for these self-produced political commentary programs presented on YouTube or X or Meta are introduced to these new voices via clips that have been shared on social media platforms.

Let me illustrate the power of social media in the age of streaming content with a scenario that should seem all too familiar with your social media habits.

You may choose Facebook as your favorite social media platform. While scrolling your feed you see that one of your friends has shared a five-minute clip of Megyn Kelly explaining an aspect of the "hush money" trial against Donald Trump that you had never heard on cable or broadcast news. You love the clip and you share it on your Facebook page. You then want to know more about this Megyn Kelly Show because the last you heard from her she was leaving Fox News and you weren't sure what ever ended up happening with her. You find her show on YouTube and you subscribe so you can catch her next program and before you know it, you're a regular viewer.

Do you see what just happened?

You saw a message promoted to you on a social media platform recommended by someone you trust. You consumed it, helped distribute it, and then became a direct consumer of the product yourself. This is how content (messaging) rapidly spreads and it also demonstrates how audiences grow through what is tantamount to free advertising through the age-old sampling process. You see a sample of the product recommended to you from within your friend's circle of influence. You like it. You become a customer. You share the free sample with your own circle of influence.

This is all standard fare when it comes to social media content. The missing factor that blows through the old dinosaur business model is the fact that the promotion for this YouTube product was executed on one of YouTube's competitor's platforms. You learned about and became the customer of a YouTube show while "watching" content on Facebook. It's like seeing an advertisement and receiving a targeted, free sample of a Fox News show while watching MSNBC. That would never happen, but it happens routinely in the streaming/social media universe. Further, Megyn Kelly can deliver her live or taped content across all these platforms simultaneously. In fact, she's encouraged to do so.

It's counter to anything the big networks would ever do.

So, this may explain how individual, democratized content creators can succeed on these platforms like YouTube, but how does any of this contribute to *defeating* the legacy media's monopoly, gatekeeping tactics? You may think that just because a show does well on YouTube it doesn't directly make an impact on the way networks continue to propagandize their audience with their slanted political coverage, and, you may be right. But let's look at what's really happening here.

Back to Megyn Kelly, who, if you'll remember, was rejected by NBC News as a ratings failure and a politically problematic employee. As you may have guessed, Megyn had the last laugh. In July 2024, her channel garnered 116.8 million views, surpassing the 78 million views that the official NBC News channel received on the same platform.

YouTube is the number one streaming service for video content, including political news content. And on that platform, in the middle of the presidential election - in a month that had the post-debate storyline, the assassination attempt storyline, the RNC convention storyline, the J.D .Vance VP pick storyline, and the Kamala-coup storyline -

Megyn Kelly absolutely trounced NBC News. It wasn't even close. And Kelly, with her single, one-hour program has a staff, budget, and production expenses significantly smaller than the venerable, legacy media brand.

This entire new paradigm for content creation and information delivery turned the entire, existing news media business model inside out, with individuals skipping the gatekeepers and making an impact on the national conversation. This entire confluence erupted right in the middle of the 2024 election cycle. Through all of the misinformation narratives promoted by the legacy corporate brands detailed in Part 2 of this book, the people knew they were being deceived and they voted with their feet - and eyeballs.

For the first time, 2024 offered the American voter a very real and legitimate alternative to the Democrat-media complex and we chose the alternative. And Trump utilized our choice to his benefit. Streaming on social media made all the difference. The medium influenced not just the message, but influenced the messengers. *We* got to pick the winners and losers. It changed everything.

We are now the media.

Chapter Sixteen - We Are Now The Media

"My message to Elon Musk is: BULLSHIT. You're not the media!" - Jim VandeHei, CEO/co-founder of *Axios*

"Yeah, whatever lmao. You are the media now. And legacy media know it." - Elon Musk responding to VandeHei on X

It was November 21st, less than three weeks after the 2024 presidential election, and Jim VandeHei was not very pleased. The journalist/entrepreneur/multi-millionaire-mogul was delivering a speech at the National Press Club in Washington DC and he railed against the rise of "Citizen Journalism" and the suggestion that something, *anything* might be broken in his beloved profession. You've got to wonder why he was so *angry*, though. After all, he was receiving an award from his esteemed colleagues at the Press Club.

The fancy DC occasion and black-tie affair was *The Fourth Estate Awards.* The dinner and gala raises money for the National Press Club Institute which, "provides training that equips journalists with skills and standards to inform the public, provides career support for journalists, and provides scholarships to aspiring journalists," according to the gala's invite. And there was VandeHei getting an award at a charity dinner for which his company, *Axios*, provided Diamond Level sponsorship to the tune of $45,000. Also noteworthy: The other Diamond Level, $45,000 sponsor of the gala was Al Jazeera Media Network (wholly owned by the Qatar government) and one of the other major award winners was, (surely coincidentally) Wael Al-Dahdouh, Al Jazeera's Gaza bureau chief who reported all year on the Israel/Gaza war. *It was completely objective and without any sort of political bias of course.*

Despite the altruistic and aspirational setting, the glamorous red carpet, paparazzi, and the trappings that go with "DC Awards Season" (which is actually a thing, believe it or not) Mr. VandeHei, one of the top honorees, was really, really angry. Instead of your standard humble acceptance speech that one would expect at one of these things, VandeHei used his allotted time to attack the notion that journalists, reporters, and media moguls (like VandeHei) had in some ways failed at their fundamental task: To report the truth. He was mostly indignant over the lack of influence the media suffered during the election year. As we explored in the previous chapter, the American people had bypassed the gatekeepers. And Mr. VandeHei, one of those gatekeepers, was pretty pissed about it.

"I hate this damn debate about like, 'Oh, we don't need the media.' Like, it is not true! Think about what makes this -I love this country, I'm a beneficiary of this country," VandeHei began, his energy, passion and tone elevating each line he delivered.

"But there's something about the country, there's something about it, right? There's something about freedom, capitalism, the animal spirits of democracy. But at the core of that is maybe transparency, maybe a free press, maybe the ability to do your job without worrying to go to jail. Maybe the ability to sit in a war zone and tell people what's actually happening so they're not just looking at distortion, matters. It matters profoundly. It's why-, it's not like we just love getting up at 3 or 4 in the morning doing this every single day. Like we do it because we love it. We do it because it matters. The work that we do matters."

Yeah, sure. But, the fact that VandeHei also benefited to the tune of tens of millions of dollars doesn't hurt either. And I couldn't find any account of Mr. VandeHei reporting from a war zone, he *hires* reporters to do that.

VandeHei, by all accounts, is an American success story.

Born right before the Watergate scandal hit the pages of *The Washington Post*, the Oshkosh, Wisconsin native graduated from the University of Wisconsin-Oshkosh with a double major in journalism and political science. He started his career in journalism by covering sports for his hometown newspaper and working at a local weekly, *the Brillion News*. Recognizing that his current career path would eventually lead to a fulfilling yet not quite as profitable life covering the Green Bay Packers and the fans who love them, he decided to move to Washington DC and cover the nation's second favorite sport: Politics.

During the Clinton era, he landed his first job in DC working for Inside Washington Publishers and *Inside the New Congress*, a newsletter focusing on the incoming Newt Gingrich-led Republican Congress. He then joined *Roll Call* in 1997, where he broke significant stories like the affairs of House Speaker-elect Bob Livingston and the formal planning of Bill Clinton's impeachment by Republicans. After *Roll Call*, VandeHei became a national political reporter for The *Wall Street Journal* in 2000, covering Congress and the White House. Two years later, in 2002, he joined *The Washington Post*, where he continued to cover Congress, the 2004 presidential campaign, and the White House.

Let's pause the bio here for a second. Have you noticed something about the business of political journalism in Washington DC?

He arrived in town in 1995 and by 2002 he had already worked for four different companies lasting barely two years at each gig. This kind of "gig hopping" may be normal now, but do you know any profession other than the news media with this kind of behavior back in the 90s? To be clear, the only way you make the contacts and build the relationships to go from working at a newsletter publication to *Roll Call* to the *Wall Street Journal* to *The Washington Post* in such a short time is spending a good chunk of it schmoozing. And that's the reality of a place like Washington and a business like the media. Everybody's working the guy or gal next to them and trying to angle for their next big thing.

You would think that getting a gig covering congress at *The Washington Post* just seven years after covering Wisconsin sports in Oshkosh would've been incredibly satisfying and fulfilling for our young protagonist, but you'd be wrong. Jim VandeHei had set his sights much higher.

In 2006, VandeHei left *The Washington Post* to co-found *Politico. Politico* quickly became known for its aggressive, fast-paced coverage of politics and policy, significantly altering the landscape of political journalism. Under his leadership as executive editor and co-founder, *Politico* expanded its influence - particularly with its digital platform - becoming one of the go-to sources for political news. One could argue that the advent of *Politico* forever altered the way politics was reported on in America.

In 2006, old-school newspaper operations were still quite skeptical of this new fad known as the Internet. They didn't quite understand how to make money on the digital landscape and they still operated on a timeline of newspaper deadlines and morning editions. *Politico* changed all that. They operated on the 24/7 up-to-the-moment digital landscape. An article that got huge traffic was just as (if not more) valuable than the circulation numbers of their local print edition.

Politico was founded at the perfect time to harness America's appetite for news *right now*. And because they were new and formed in the digital age they didn't have to fight institutional stagnation that had festered at the newspaper and magazine offices down the block. If *Politico* wanted to try something new and different, they could. And they did. And *Politico* was a huge success.

Ten years later, VandeHei was ready to move on again. It was time to exit *Politico* and start a brand-new venture funded by deep-pocketed investors. Because… Journalism. When he left *Politico* he seemed to lament the very digital news universe he helped create. He wrote an article in *The Information* titled "Journalists Are Killing Journalism," where he lamented the state of the news business, particularly focusing on the obsession with clicks.

VandeHei criticized the industry's move towards chasing clicks over quality journalism. He argued that this has led to a focus on sensationalism, quick, shallow content, and clickbait, which he believed was degrading the quality of news. He expressed concern that the pressure to generate more clicks has led journalists to prioritize stories with high viral potential over substantive reporting. This shift, VandeHei noted, undermines the traditional values of journalism like depth, accuracy, and context.

He described how the industry's business model had evolved into one where traffic numbers dictate editorial decisions, leading to a "race to the bottom" in terms of content quality. This, he suggested, was a significant factor in the decline of trust in media. VandeHei called for a return to journalism's roots, emphasizing the need for news organizations to focus on providing valuable, well-researched content that informs rather than just entertains. He advocated for a new business model that values quality over quantity, suggesting that there might be a market for such journalism if done correctly.

We'll leave others to comment at length about the hypocrisy and lack of self-awareness VandeHei had to possess to leave *Politico* because he feared the new industry had devolved into chasing clicks, ignoring in-depth reporting, and valuing high-quantity of content versus high-quality journalism - considering this is pretty much a summation of *exactly what Politico was at its founding.* VandeHei and his *Politico* co-founder Mike Allen left to form a brand new venture which, one would assume, would address the deeply held concerns VandeHei expressed in his "Farewell Address" from *Politico* .

Enter: *Axios*

In 2016, VandeHei, along with Allen and Roy Schwartz, co-founded *Axios*. The company aimed to provide readers with quick, digestible news updates, focusing on "smart brevity." "Smart brevity" became such a watch-cry at *Axios* that it became the title of a book co-authored by the *Axios* founders. "Smart Brevity: The Power of Saying More with Less" was published in 2022. The book advocated for a communication style that prioritizes brevity and clarity, especially in an age where attention spans are short and information overload is common. It delved into the "Smart Brevity" method developed at *Axios*, which focuses on delivering essential information quickly and effectively.

Does anything in the *Axios* "smart brevity" model sound like it solves the problems in the media VandeHei lamented in his navel-gazing article in "The Information"? What was the name of the article again...? Oh, yes: "Journalists are Killing Journalism." How did he put it again?

"The news industry has become a disgusting, click-obsessed commoditizer of content. It's not about informing people but titillating them."

And...

"We're now in the age of the headline, where the story — not just the lead but the entire narrative — is secondary to getting you to click on the link. Depth is dead."

And...

"The best journalists are spending less time on stories that matter and more time trying to divine what will go viral. This is not just bad for democracy but bad for our souls."

And...

*"The business model has morphed into something unrecognizable from what we learned in J-school. It's no

longer about the story but about the traffic. And that's a tragedy."

Yes, that's what he said. And then he formed *Axios* which was entirely designed to emphasize brevity in the form of clickable headlines and short bullet points to deliver just the nuggets of information *Axios* decides the reader needs to know. In fact, *Axios* went so far to include a self-indulgent and arrogant summation with each little digestible semi-article with the header "Why it matters" to literally tell a reader why the article they are about to read matters and what matters about it.

Naturally, one assumes that a busy person skimming their news feed or articles or the *Axios* newsletter delivered to their inbox read the "Why it matters" header and accompanying bullet points. Then, the busy person would move on because, after all, they just got their one-line executive summary. They now know "why it matters" so why waste time with any more information?

Wow, Jim! Great job bringing us all back to the roots of in-depth reporting and analysis. Also, Jim, thank you for taking it upon yourself to tell your readers why something matters in the first place. Is there a more arrogant and self-serving example of blatant editorializing than a writer or editor telling you with a bolded sub-headline the only take-aways that *really matter* about the article you're about to read? They must presume the reader can't possibly be relied upon to digest facts and then use their own intellect, wisdom, and life experience to determine what *really matters* in the article or, more importantly, why it matters *to the reader.*

No, Mr VandeHei must do that for you, lest you lead yourself to the conclusion Mr. VandeHei doesn't want you to reach.

Now, back to Jim's acceptance speech at the black-tie gala his company paid $45,000 to help throw:

"Everything we do is under fire. Elon Musk sits on Twitter every day or X today saying like, "We are the media. You are the media." My message to Elon Musk is: Bullshit! You're not the media, you having a blue checkmark, a Twitter handle and 300 words of cleverness doesn't make you a reporter any more than me looking at your head, and seeing that you have a brain and telling you have an awesome set of tools makes me a damn neurosurgeon, right?

"Like what we do, what journalists do, what you did in Mississippi, what Al-Jazeera does in the Middle East. You don't proclaim yourself to be a reporter. Like this nonsense, like being a reporter is hard. Really hard. You have to care. You have to do the hard work. You have to get up every single day and say, "I want to get to the closest approximation of the truth without any fear, without any favoritism." You

don't do that by popping off on Twitter. You don't do that by having an opinion. You do it by doing the hard work."

Clearly, VandeHei, speaking on behalf of the entire profession he helped to transform (and perhaps destroy) was quite indignant that Musk was suggesting that lowly amateurs, mere mortals, without even the benefit of a Journalism degree could perhaps contribute to the live, real-time media landscape we are now all currently living in. He hated the idea of "Citizen Journalism." Musk, meanwhile, represented citizen journalism in its purest form.

By purchasing Twitter, rebranding it as "X," and loosening the notoriously oppressive "moderation" and censorship regime instituted by the former ownership, Musk had created a free, wide-open playing field for independent voices to report, comment, and amplify thoughts and ideas based on their personal expertise and influence. VandeHei rightly saw this new approach to narrative building and content creation as an existential threat to the kingdoms of influence he had created.

So what *is* citizen journalism?

Citizen journalism, in essence, refers to the practice where ordinary individuals, rather than professional journalists, collect, report, analyze, and disseminate news and information. This form of journalism leverages the widespread availability of digital tools like smartphones, social media, and blogging platforms to share eyewitness accounts, personal stories, or investigative reports directly with the public.

Andrew Breitbart is considered the Godfather of citizen journalism as he leveraged the power and visibility of his websites to promote individuals like James O'Keefe, Ben Shapiro, Kurt Schlichter, and the author of the book you're reading right now.

Breitbart gave rise to the citizen journalist movement by encouraging individuals to send him videos captured on smartphones of news events, as well as interactions with elected officials. During the Tea Party movement of 2010, the citizen journalist with a smartphone exploded with several lawmakers behaving badly and captured for the nation to see.

Rep. Bob Etheridge (D-NC) was caught physically confronting two young men who approached him on a Washington, D.C., street to ask if he supported the "Obama agenda." Etheridge grabbed one of the men by the wrist and demanded to know who they were. Breitbart promoted the video on his site and Ethridge lost re-election. Rep. Phil Hare (D-IL) was also a casualty of Breitbart's citizen journalism campaign. During a town hall meeting in Quincy, Illinois, when asked by a Tea Party activist about the constitutionality of the Obamacare bill, Hare responded, "I don't worry about the Constitution on this, to be honest." Hare was also sent to an early retirement that November.

I know these stories because as Breitbart's video editor that year, I helped produce, publish, and promote these videos. It was the dawn of citizen journalism and it was glorious.

At a Tax Day Tea Party rally in Washington, D.C., on April 15, 2010, Andrew asked attendees to hold up their cameras and cell phones, demonstrating the power of new media and citizen journalism.

He said:

"It's time for a new media revolution, and you are it! You are the media! Hold up your phones! Hold up your cameras! This is the future of media! This is how we are going to fight the lies, the misinformation, and the propaganda of the mainstream media. We are now the media!"

The gesture was a galvanizing symbol of Breitbart's push for grassroots media activism and his belief that technology empowered individuals to challenge the narratives set by traditional media outlets. Fast-forward to 2024. With the support and backing of the richest man on the planet, Breitbart's vision has come to fruition.

We *are* now the media, indeed. And there's no going back.

Ever.

The End.

Acknowledgments

On June 23, 2015, I got down on one knee and with a tear coming down my eye I asked Meredith Dake to bless me with her hand in marriage. She agreed to marry this divorced man with four children and my life was suddenly complete. She is my daily inspiration and the voice in my head always guiding me in the right direction. She is my life and I couldn't have written this book (or done anything else for that matter) without her. If this book makes any coherent sense, has proper grammar and is not riddled with misspellings and typos, it's because of Meredith Dake.

My children, Quinn, Veronica, Christian and EJ, have been the primary motivation for everything I do. Before every life decision I ask, "Will this be the right thing for the kids?" and that always puts me on the path of a good choice. I hope my work makes you proud.

Few people have the opportunity to meet a person (other than their spouse) who forever changes the course of their life. That person, for me, was Andrew Breitbart. Thank you, Andrew. God, we miss you.

Kurt Schlichter has been an invaluable friend, advisor, and a rock of consistent advocacy since we both embarked on this strange new world of political commentary and media. His advice and guidance in the process of writing this book was priceless and I only fear how many drinks I'm going to have to buy him to make it up to him.

My work family at WMAL: Without my Program Director Bill Hess, I'd still sound like an amateur talking to a few hundred people on the Internet. He sanded off my rough edges and helped me fool everyone into thinking I'm a professional broadcaster. He is the best. My Executive Producer Heather Hunter has helped me find my voice and knows just how to push me to make me better. Her instincts for news and compelling talk radio is unmatched. She's the sister I never had. Julie Gunlock makes me laugh more than anyone I know and she is the perfect person to have a public conversation with at 5 AM. Patrice Onwuka is a gifted communicator and her effervescence picks me up right at the end of the week when I need it most. Mercedes Schlapp is wise, savvy, smart, beautiful and a reliable confidant. Her advice and support is irreplaceable.

My work family at Townhall: Jonathan Garthwaite and Storm Paglia lead us with intelligence, firm but subtle guidance and good humor. In the Internet news business, it's rare to feel secure with your leadership but they pull it off. My Producer, Kevin MacMahon is a genius. He helped this "Gen X'er" find his video-streaming voice and delivery. I'm forever grateful for our daily interactions.

My agent and career advisor Heather Cohen took a chance on me and I am forever grateful for her wise advice.

Thank you to Chris Stigall for always making me laugh. Mark Levin for always making me better. Hugh Hewitt for always reminding me that class and courtesy will always be remembered. Chris Plante for the use of "Morning Joke" to describe the Joe and Mika Show... *everyone in my business steals from Chris Plante, I'm one of the few radio hosts who cop to it.* Mollie Hemingway for being a warrior every day. Brent Bozell and the team at Media Research Center. Gov. Scott Walker, Jessica Jensen, Spencer Brown and the team at Young America's Foundation. Sarah Smith Zwirecki for guiding my social media strategy and for advising me on pretty much everything, including home landscaping.

Sean Salter for his mesmerizing art work on the cover of this book.

I have been so fortunate to work with and become friends with so many smart and talented thought-leaders, broadcasters and writers that I hesitate to begin listing them lest I leave someone out, If that's you, I am truly sorry.

Thank you to my father, Dennis Paul O'Connor, Sr. Dad, you gave me my voice and taught me how to communicate with wit and grace. Thank you to my stepmother, Jann O'Connor, who kept me grounded, encouraged my love for arts and entertainment, and has selflessly cared for the man she loves, my dad, in these final, difficult years.

Larry O'Connor
Annapolis, Maryland
January 2025

About Larry O'Connor

Larry O'Connor is a radio talk show host on Washington, D.C.'s WMAL, where he hosts the morning drive-time show O'Connor & Company. He also hosts LARRY, a daily, streaming video show and podcast for Townhall Media, reaching several million viewers per month. Larry is a frequent guest host for nationally syndicated hosts Mark Levin, Dennis Miller, and Hugh Hewitt.

Larry's columns have appeared on Townhall, The Washington Times, Hot Air, The Federalist, Washington Free Beacon, and Andrew Breitbart's trailblazing original websites Big Hollywood, Big Government, and BreitbartTV.

While with Andrew Breitbart, O'Connor became a trailblazer himself by creating one of the first live, daily internet radio programs/podcasts, which quickly attracted a large and loyal following. The online program led to his high-profile guest-hosting appearances and, eventually, his current job on WMAL—one of the highest-rated and most influential talk radio stations in America. He was the first online radio host to successfully transition to a major-market radio career.

Before radio, Larry was the general manager of the Shubert Theatre in Los Angeles, where he oversaw the American premiere of Andrew Lloyd Webber's Sunset Blvd., starring Glenn Close. He also worked on major productions, including Ragtime, Rent, Beauty and the Beast, Chicago, Cats, and A Chorus Line. During his theatre career, Larry worked with Sir Ian McKellen, Kelsey Grammar, Christine Baranski, Neil Patrick Harris, Adam Lambert, and, regrettably, Val Kilmer.

Larry is married to Meredith Dake-O'Connor, and they have four children: Quinn, a UCLA graduate and theatrical stage manager/producer; Veronica, an ensign in the United States Navy and graduate of the Naval Academy; Christian, a sophomore at UCSD; and EJ, a special needs high school senior.

Made in the USA
Middletown, DE
01 April 2025

73523850R00175